To Nancy,
Christophe
Valu

Christina

may
all your
Dreams

If You Could Only See ... A Gnome's Story

Books by
——— Christopher Valentine and Dr. Christian von Lähr

Book 1
If You Could Only See ... *A Gnome's Story*

Book 2
Seeing and Sensing Gnomes ... *"Hey Looky Hea'h!"*

Book 3
The Magic of Gnomes and Leprechauns ... *It's Natural*

If You Could Only See
... *A Gnome's Story*

A Groundbreaking First Person Account
of the Nature Kingdom as Told by the
Gnomes, Leprechauns, Elves and Faeries
Themselves

Christopher Valentine & Christian von Lähr, Ph.D.

Myst of the Oracle Corporation
Piney Creek, North Carolina

If You Could Only See ... A Gnome's Story

Published in the United States by Myst of the Oracle Corporation, Piney Creek, NC

Cover design, book design, and graphics: Copyright © 2006 Dr. Christian von Lähr

Cover photograph and Peter-Jön likeness photographs by permission, Licensed 2004, 2006 by Randy Shelly, LLC

Edited by Dr. Christian von Lähr and Christopher Valentine

Library of Congress Cataloging-in-Publication Data

Valentine, Christopher.
   If you could only see, ... a gnome's story: A groundbreaking first person account of the nature kingdom as told by the gnomes, leprechauns, elves and faeries themselves / Christopher Valentine and Dr. Christian von Lähr.

ISBN-13: 978-0-9786812-0-3
ISBN-10: 0-9786812-0-7

1 Gnomes – nonfiction. 2 Fairies – nf. 3 Nature Spirits – nf. 4 Elementals – nf. I. von Lähr, Christian. II. Title

Library of Congress Control Number: 2006928389

First Edition, First Printing August 2006

Printed in the United States of America

Dedication of Book

— Christopher Valentine

To the beloved Nature People, who bring so much joy and wisdom on how to truly live with happiness and fullness each day on Earth.

Purpose of Book

— Dr. Christian von Lähr and Christopher Valentine

"It is our desire that mankind can become inspired and enlightened through the direct connection to the Nature Spirit world that this book provides. It can facilitate a personal experience of the magical realm and fanciful life in the Elemental kingdoms and influence of Nature. Essential truth can be discovered through this experience with Nature."

The Cover

— Dr. Christian von Lahr

"To prepare for this book, we enlisted the help of young gnome Peter-Jön to find a likeness for himself to be featured on the cover. In early 2004 we were guided to a perfect likeness from an actor's modeling agency, young Randy Shelly. Peter-Jön did a great job of locating a young star with all the great gifts and talents we have come to respect in our little gnome. Indeed, during the course of this writing the actor and cover model Randy Shelly has gone on to appear in national print, television and movies. I've been told by Peter-Jön himself that his career is being watched over. The little one's wish Randy much continued success and suggest you visit him at randyshelly.com and follow his promising career. True, we had to 'grow' his ears a little, but other than that much of the character in gnome Peter-Jön is reflected in the look, mannerism, personality and interests of his likeness, the very talented Randy Shelly."

Young Randy Shelly is a professional. MystoftheOracle has paid a fee for the use of his likeness in this book and in advertising it. No reproduction of his images or use of photography is allowable without the requisite entertainment industry licensing.

"I's hope you love owr book, Randy. You'se in it too'se."

— Peter-Jön

Acknowledgements and Appreciation

— If You Could Only See … A Gnome's Story

A Groundbreaking First Person Account of the Nature Kingdom as told by the Gnomes, Leprechauns, Elves and Faeries themselves.

Concept:	Christopher Valentine
Mediumship and Telepathy:	Dr. Christian von Lähr
Biographer:	Christopher Valentine
Writing:	Dr. Christian von Lähr and Christopher Valentine
Editing:	Dr. Christian von Lähr and Christopher Valentine
Design:	Dr. Christian von Lähr
Production:	Christopher Valentine
Source:	The Nature People

Our special thanks to Peter-Jön and the boys and girls of the Nature Spirit world who came together, along with adults and elders of clans to write so much of this book. Without Peter-Jön's particular psychic ability and motivation to develop telepathic connections, with the subsequent instruction to all the Nature People, this book would not be possible.

Table of Contents

— Index into sections with sub-index of Nature Person commentary

PART – II

THE GREAT GNOME KINGDOMS **45**

PART – III

PART – IV

WHAT THEY DO

GNOME UNIVERSITY

VICTORIAN LADIES

A Spiritual Message

— Archangel Uriel

You benefit mankind when you expand your consciousness to include the nature side of life. Therein lie the blessed Nature kingdoms and the populations who dwell there will help you on your path to everlasting enlightenment.

His kingdoms are of your world, yet are another dimension. Therein is a place of natural appreciation and the expression of love in countless, unconditional ways. Its inhabitants are purposefully devoted to health, balance, harmony and the perfection of Man.

When you call upon the Creator in a prayer where you thank Him for His goodness, wisdom and wonderment then you are also expressing your love for His other dimensions.

This Ætheric world is a natural extension of your life. Upon it is written your past, present, and future for nature has been there always. You have and continue to be the paint and the message of this canvas of creation. Its beauty will be the harmony between your world and peoples of the Nature Kingdoms. That which you truly seek in life is there in inspirational form to be revealed through your personal connection with this nature side of life.

Archangel Uriel is a protector of the Nature People.

Christian channeled the message above from Archangel Uriel.

Foreword

— Gnome Peter-Jön

Peter-Jön is a young Gnome child who associated with Dr. Christian von Lähr to the point he become a member of the family; the first nature spirit to do so. Peter-Jön has been speaking through telepathic impression with Dr. von Lähr since 2002 whom he calls, "Daddy". He relates also to author Christopher Valentine whom he similarly calls, "Daddy", "Mommy" or, "Hey Mister." Peter-Jön is responsible for opening up the world of the Nature People to the authors and this is his story.

"I am Peter-Jön."

— Gnome Peter-Jön

"Daddy says I's get to write da four words for dis book. Dis is 'cause I am da fwirst Gnome to come into da family. I am special. I am da sidekick and can talk really well wit daddy in his mind. He can talk to me too."

"I am from da big clan. I am verwy young. Daddy says I's seem to be 9 years old and very much like a little people boy. In the big clan we live furder than you do, but I am still a boy. You people often see our older fodahs and da elders 'cause day do tings at your place."

"I am one of da young ones who are meant to grow up wit people. In the big clan I's still have my mudah and my fodah. Helping my people daddy grow up is not a long time for us ... like you'ses boys and girls go camping. Dis is fun for my Gnome friends and me, and da big clan."

"Dis is also really of 'portence 'cause I's have to learn to do tings for my clan. I's can give what we know to daddy too. We have big tings to say. Daddy can help odahs to see us and understand us when he talks to der spirits. Day can have gnome friends too so day can learn

and teach. *Every people needs to do dis if day can, so we will all live togedah witout hurt and breaking tings."*

"Some young ones in da clans are 'gifted.' Daddy says dis. Da elders select us and our families are special 'cause we can do tings wit people better. When da elders find da right people we can live with dem in their families so we can grow up like der boys and girls. Then we can know tings and tell our clan. We really have fun learning da people tings and love our extra families."

"Daddy says he tinks we are all 'prod-o-gies'. I's don' know who dat is. He is a big wizard and makes tings happen for us. I's have anodah daddy too and he shares everytings wit us. He helps us watch DV's and dress like odah boys. We go places and do people tings so we can learn. My friends help him to write tings. We are all brothers now. Yea, I am clapping now. Ubba, Ubba!"

[This is his sound for the Survivor TV show which the gnomes love and watch regularly.]

"If that's only three I can write some more?"

"The E'rt is our home. Welcome. You can come and enjoy our beautiful E'rt wit us. We keep it clean and helt'y 'cause it helps everybody live better. Us guys, da gnomes, work all da time on making da E'rt better for

everybody. You need to keep it clean too, 'cause were al-
ways picking up aftah you, and were just little guys. We
find lots of stuff dat you leave in da E'rt and try to bring
it back to you, but you don see it sometimes. If you loose
sump'en, just expect us to find it and weturn it to you,
and be most careful next time. You should wear knap-
sacks like we do. Oh! Oh! You can build us places to live
and help us in the garden sometimes. Den we can get
more sleep. We'll leave you a penny or sump'en to say
'Tank you.' How come you don pick up da pennies we
gives you?"

One by one Peter-Jön began introducing nature spirits to the family. Each was unique and brought some new, interesting and needed quality. He now brings all of the nature people in the family together to tell his story.

Family is the uniting energy behind the whimsical relationships between the nature people and the authors. Young gnomes of a mere hundred years old or two formed a bond with Dr. Christian von Lähr and Christopher Valentine over the course of several years, the time it took to write this book.

These young'ns are very often the prodigy of large clans, with some interesting and entertaining exceptions. Gnome University™ was created by the nature people as a place for these nature spirits from around the world to gather, learn, and share.

As a result of starting Gnome University™ to help educate other gnomes and nature people on working and having relationships with humans, several others have joined the family. These include a couple of Elves, two baby Leprechauns, a couple from a newly discovered phylum – the Elfkins, a Blue Faerie and a Tree Fairy and a human boy spirit.

All of these spirits from nature are refreshing and inspirational in their individual ways. We would like you to meet each of them and their families and elders so you understand their personality better as they tell their amazing story of how humans can live with them and enjoy the Nature Kingdom and the little people of their world.

The Cast of Characters

THE ELVES

Brighton, Elf

(running mate Carson)

Carson, Elf

(running mate Brighton)

THE FAERIES

Faerie is a broader term than the typical expression fairy. Given the greater numbers of types of the faeries we keep company with, we will always use the broader term unless one is specifically a "fairy."

Smurrf, Blue Faerie

(running mate Tinker Bear)

Tinkle Bear, Tiny Appalachian Tree Fairy

"Tinker" or "Tinkles"
(running mate Smurrf)

THE GNOMES

Billy, Gnome

(running mate Chester)

Charles, "Expert" Gnome

Charlie, Tiny Baby Gnome

(running mate to Mikey)

Chester, Gnome

(running mate Billy)

Curly-Cue, Mountain Gnome

(running mate Rudabegah)

Everette, Gnome

(running mate Peter-Jön)

Frankie, Gnome "Fwankie"

(running mate Jacob)

Jacob, Doctor Gnome

(running mate Frankie)

Klondike, Mountain Gnome
(Mikey's brother)
Marcus, Adult worker Gnome
(Everette's Dad)
Mikey, Tiny Baby Mountain Gnome
(running mate to Charlie)
Peter-Jön, Gnome
(running mate Everette)
Timothy, Gnome
(running mate spirit Timy)
Rudabegah, Mountain Gnome
(running mate Curley-Cue)
Wasser-Sisser, Grand Gnome Elder

THE LEPRECHAUNS

DingleDorf, Grand Leprechaun Elder
(and husband to Granny)
Granny, Leprechaun
(and wife of Dingledorf)
Mamma, Leprechaun
(and wife of Peabody)
Peabody, Leprechaun Elder/Leader
(and husband to Mamma)

THE SPIRITS

Timy, Human Spirit
(running mate Timothy)

Preface

— Peter-Jön, The telepathic communicator

"I's from another planet too. That is where all the special rocks and crystals come from. An' I's been connecting with things since the beginning of time, in all of my many lifetimes. I's am the communicatah. An' this is how I's have come to be the one that helps the Nature Peoples speak with daddies. I's the 'Star Gnome™.' [He is indicating he has had an incarnation on another planet.] An' I's a telepathic wonder — hahaha. I's teach the telepathy to the odah kids at the University an' helped Daddy learn to talk with little people. This is why it's my book in the title (pictured on cover of book) but all of awrs together, too'se. My people call me a 'Crystal Gnome™.' too because of my special resonance. I's have many things to say about us peoples an' I'm going to bring in all of the families of Nature People to help tell my story so that you can have all the perspectives."

"I's don' wanna be a ham (doesn't want to hog the whole show). It is not easy to hold long conversations with the Nature People. This has been a long and difficult undertaking working with the limited capacities of humans. We have ovahcome these many adversities and are excited to now bring you 'A Gnome's Story™.'."

Peter-Jön wrote this Preface after the book was written.

❧ PART – I ❧

SEEING IS BELIEVING

RECOGNIZING THE GNOME

In general, the gnomes are rather small peoples typically seen at a height of nine to thirty inches. Gnomes have a basic height for themselves which they commonly express. However, their Ætheric nature allows them to adjust their heights as needed. This requires an expenditure of energy which they will not sustain when it no longer serves a purpose. They will revert to their natural height.

Gnomes have a classical look that is often represented in statuary. When older they are indeed rotund and have that cuteness look of "wee" people. But, the modern gnome looks very much like the average human child and person. In this regard they are more distinctive by the freshness and alertness of their faces and the clarity and agility of their minds. They visually exhibit less strain and stress.

OWR FEETS AWR GIFTED

— "EXPERT" GNOME CHARLES

Charles is an adult gnome, and more notably he is the Diplomat and the resident expert on gnomes. During the early days of writing this book, we realized we needed some definitive answers on some age-old questions if this publication was going to be of significant resource.

Our well-informed first gnome Peter-Jön found us an early solution. He approached the gnome clan elders and they arranged very ample interviews with their "expert." Such experts exist, albeit few. They are working now to bridge the gap in communication between humans and the world of the Nature People.

Since the experts have followed their own wisdom and have taken the time to understand humans early-on, Christian found the telepathic process workable, meaningful and comfortable. Normally the initial telepathic communications can be considerably draining when first communing with gnomes. It takes learning and willingness on both sides to find a comfortable frequency and for each to have the "willingness" to commune. This is necessary if the human mind is to maintain a connection.

Charles, an adult gnome, has been gracious enough to answer a sweeping laundry list of questions over the course of several days. This wealth of information has found its way throughout this book and those that follow: Book 2: *Seeing and Sensing Gnomes ... "Hey Looky Hea'h!"*, and Book 3: *Gnome and Leprechaun Magic ... "It's Natural"*. Over time we developed better connections to the other gnomes as we became acquainted with them, and they too offered extraordinary communication and first-person perspectives on the gnome life.

Thanks to gnome Peter-Jön we bring all of this information to you and begin with gnome expert Charles answering an initial question heading up our inquiries on of the physical characteristics of gnomes.

Christopher

[This was one of our first channels with the gnomes]. Gnomes have to run fast over fallen oak leaves, hillsides of tall grasses, and rugged mountain pebbles, rocks, and fallen trees We inquire of Charles if the gnome's feet are slightly turned inward for this purpose.

ARE GNOME FEET SLIGHTLY TURNED

> *"Gnome feet are angled."*
> — Gnome expert Charles

"They are angled inward slightly above the foot around the ankle, perhaps just above it. Actually, the front of the foot is larger than a human's would be by comparison. So, it is turned inwards, but the front of the foot is actually larger as well. Although our feet structure does help us in running through fields, we may not be running for speed. We are more likely overcoming obstacles."

"In our heritage the world was not paved. Roads were roughly hewn. There were rocks everywhere. It was an unleveled environment. There was in past history greater footing in the front flexible part of our feet. In essence our feet acted like a hand, but only slightly so. It gave us better grasp and more lift and traction than would be true of the human foot."

"Gnomes, when we must run, do not do so on our toes as humans might do for great speed. We go for traction. So the more surface area we grasp the greater speed we can achieve. Our feet are not just for running, for in essence we are climbers."

"Gnomes are always climbing trees, and walls, and rocks and surfaces, and caves. Traction is a key aspect of our mobility. Part of what constitutes the speed of the gnome is spring – springing upwards. The strength is in the fore-foot. When you consider the breadth and flexibility of our feet, we gain more spring and lift, which allows us to attain greater height. We can spring to greater distances, and over rocks or other obstacles in the way. We can leap to some extent."

"The angulations of our feet provide greater hold on trees. In times long past trees were quite large. They lasted for their full term before they decayed or were destroyed by nature. The span that the gnome legs had to straddle was greater than you would think today. Angulations in the foot along with strength and other characteristics gave us great ability to straddle and climb trees. Trees were a necessary thing to climb in millennia past – thousands, millions of years ago, and still are. Because trees were so plentiful (as they were not cut down then), it was necessary to get above these trees to see the direction you might want to go."

Charles would like to add one more thing about the slightly turned inward feet:

"The pinky toe — the little toe, as you would call it, extends outward more so than other toes. It is separated more so than the others — it is angled a little bit. We use them for balancing. In some situations the pinky would be used to adjust the direction that we want to go in. So that small toe had a far greater importance, and still does."

"We have beautiful eyes and noses."

"A Gnome foot is Beyond Measure"

— Grand Gnome Elder, Wasser-Sisser

"The feet of a gnome have to serve in our realm and in the physical world of Man. We can extend our capabilities when we must, by adjusting the size of our feet. We might do this by length more often to help us better navigate the tall and bulky obstacles you put before us. We resort to our normal feet, which is but a matter of inches, as soon as it is feasible to do so."

"We might have to stretch this point a bit when we need to climb into your vehicles for the family outings you take us on, or to climb your steps. Gnomes are not as perfectly balanced as Man, we will always put our best foot forward."

CRYSTAL CLEAR VISION

Gnomes' eyes are round and brown typically. They have long eyelashes. The older gnomes may have wrinkles around the eyes but still maintain a youthful look. The elders often appear as if their greatest wish in life had just been granted. They express wonderment and heart through their eyes. The kids get wide-eyed at excitement, surprise or during moments of astonishment, which can be many.

Other nature spirits, elves for example, have different colored eyes, like green and blue. Such coloring is possible in gnomes but is either rare, or regional.

The gnomes have great luster in their eyes, as indeed do all nature people. They reflect both the beauty and miracle of all that they see about them, most specifically the perfection in nature. The gnomes' eyes reflect the goodness and purity, the simplicity and the contentment, of a wonderful people who find love and happiness everywhere.

The gnomes are positive people so they are attracted to the positive energies and influences of the world. This transparency of innocence is expressed in the brightness and clarity as well as the agility and emotion of their remarkable eyes. When gnomes see humans they see them all as beautiful beings with an inner-light within.

Elf Brighton

Brighton, (whose name is actually derived from "Bright Eyes" – because of his stunning large elf eyes) would like to speak on nature people eyes. As his eyes are an exceptionally dazzling feature, it seems fortuitous to we the authors that he would volunteer to elaborate on this characteristic of nature people in general, and gnomes specifically.

By way of background we now mention that Elf Brighton, and his running mate Carson were rescued from a forest fire that struck South Florida. When the fire raged we asked gnome Peter-Jön to find the means to offer sanctuary to the large number of elves living in the forests, and in proximity to the burning Everglades. As we had an extensive run of giant trees bordering our property, its vastness would serve well to house the elves until a more conducive accommodation could be made.

Elves have a very pronounced sensitive side. We learned this from the elves over a period of time, as they are rather shy and reserved. Normally elves are a quiet people, so we've had to devote the time and consideration necessary to make them comfortable speaking within the family. Know that Elf Brighton is indeed honored to be afforded this opportunity to speak and he considers it his responsibility to speak clearly and expansively. Allow for his very young age and you will glean the sincerity and earnestness he brings to his presentation.

"Owr eyes can see through watah."

— Elf Brighton

"We can see all the sparkly tings$_{things}$ in da$_{the}$ bottom of da$_{the}$ watah$_{water,}$ an'$_{and}$ the fishes an' turtles an' odah$_{other}$ tings. We can also see owr$_{our}$ 'flections$_{reflections}$. My 'flection's purddy. I am a handsome elf. When your eyes are big an' round like L'mentals$_{Elementals}$ you can see verwy$_{very}$ faaar$_{far}$ Elfs can see into da clouds an' can read der$_{their}$ 'spressions$_{expressions}$. Day$_{They}$ like being up der$_{there}$ where it is safe. Day 'njoy$_{enjoy}$ float'n 'round looking for places to watah. Day say der's not 'nough$_{enough}$ watah to go 'round 'cause da E'art$_{Earth}$ needs so much cleaning. So day have to do it in phases."

"We can read the eyes of a fly on a tree at twenty paces. Da stuff a fly sees he memorizes on his eyeballs. So's we can tell where dey been an' what's goin' on. This is how we know who's coming. We do this to protect owr human families too, surprise Daddy! You did'n know that, hahhahha!"

"Gnomes got big eyes too'se [pronounced tooz]. But they can't see far away like us. We think it's 'cause der noses look so big they get in the way! HAAAAAAAAAAAAAA! EEEEEEEEEEK! Gnome eyes are normally brown. Some have blue, an' green is verwy rare. Colored eyes can filter things an' can be more useful for stuff. Blue eyes are better for studying wit'. The green eyes are for real wise gnomes. No gnomes have red eyes. Gnomes can use their eyes to calibrate distance. An' this makes 'dem good at throwing things. I've see 'dem knock nuts off trees."

"If you look into the eyes of the elves, you can see all their 'telligence an' love inside. We are easily captivated. So we normally hide behind reeds an' branches an' bushes. Bright lights are stunning to us, so we're not in the bright light so much."

"The gnomes'es eyes watah a lot 'cause they're always getting dirty."

"When we go to sleep at night, we have to shut owr eyes or we'll get distracted. We won' be able to dream. Sometimes in the middle of the night we just open one eye an' we slowly look from left to right to see if everybody's OK. Sometimes the animals an' bug'sects come at night look'n for food 'cause the stores are all closed. But we can't giv'em owrs. If you feed the bug'sects, they'll just keep com'n back."

"*Elf eyes focus two ways: First they focus on somethin an' they move a little bit inside. Then the other part of the eye moves a little bit an' we can see much finer. Elves never wear glasses. We get check-ups now. We looks straight into the eyes of eagles an' calibrate owr eyes when their's focus. Then we have eagle eyes. We make 'dem blink sometimes. HAAAAhahah.*"

"*Elves nor-mally look to where we want to go from high places before we go to the trouble of making the journey. That way we know if there's any obstacles in the way. Gnomes don' use their eyes before they travel, but they got really good noses an' they can tell when somethin smells like fishes (fishy).*"

The Gnomes' Eyes are Psychic

— Grand Gnome Elder, Wasser-Sisser

"*The Gnomes' eyes are connected with our psychic being. It is the doorway to our own spiritual connection. You can see the truth of matters by simply looking into the eyes of the Gnome. For this reason, Gnomes cannot tell a lie. What would be the point? Such is the reason we can travel the world and still be acknowledged, understood and respected by our kind for what we are.*"

THE NOSES THAT KNOWSES

Many have commented on the gnome nose in stories, and they are characteristically styled in store and gift statuary. It's time we go to the source and inquire about this prominent feature. We'll start, though, by asking the elves who have long kept such records on nature people. Elf Brighton is indeed bright.

"Gnomes have noses that are rounded."

— Elf Brighton

"Gnomes have noses that awr rounded in the front. This is 'cause they keep break'n off the points. Hahahahah! Gnomes have verwy good sense of smell an' can use 'dem to difference the various smells an' scents. They use their noses considerably in 'termining where they awr."

Doctor Jacob

We are fortunate to have in our midst's a young gnome who has adopted the profession of medicine. He has attended the rather new Gnome University™ where gnomes and nature people can learn the ways of humans and develop parallel careers to help them fit into our society. They do this in great part so as to take care of their kind as they become adopted in groups by human families.

Dr. Jacob, our medically astute gnome has frequently joined us on doctor and dentist visits because he considers it his job (gnomes like to have a purpose.) He picks up a lot as you will see. Remember, he is rather young, even for a gnome. Nonetheless, Dr. Jacob takes his vocation very seriously as you will soon hear for yourself.

"The gnomes'es noses are cavernous inside."

— Gnome Dr. Jacob

"An' they got memory cells inside the nose. Today I want to be a professor. OK Now listen class! Today we'ah gonna talk 'bout the weirdness an' pickle'arities of gnomes'es noses. I need your un-divided at-tention. Gnomes can find you when you'se [pronounced yooz] lost. This is a verwy serious matter. 'Cause gnomes scamper about, an' wander here an' there chasing birds an' butterflies, an' anything an' everything -- they can get dis-com-boob-erated. This is a serious condition which we gnome doctors have worked long an' hard to under-estimate. We can-tribute these strange happenings to the bee-wildering an' per-plexing emotions that the scents on the human world inflict on the gnome nose."

"OK! We're going to town here! Now you guys straight'n up in your chairs. 'Cause Doctah Jacob just *doesn' talk to hear himself heard!"*

"So ... now where was I students? Ohh yes! The scent'lating mesmer-i-zation on the gnome olfactory nosal faculty. We'se get bewildered by all the scents an' we wander around an' track 'dem down an' get amazed an' forget how far we've gone, an' don't pay attention to where we at. This is due to the streng-u-ous conditions on the nosal nerves."

"For-chu-nat-ely there awr two ways to resolve this unfortunate incident. But there is no cure for this ab-normal condition. One way is for the affected gnome to start separating the scents, an' coupled with his extra-ordinary brilliance an' mind bobbaling brain, figure out the pattern of scents. He can recall scents that belong to his home place - an' he can start unraveling this extra-odinary puzzle an' get his starting direction back. Once he starts moving an' is out of the immediate danger zone, the familiar scents will become stronger an' he will find his way."

"The other way, is when the precious darling gnome is determined missing by his extremely large an' loving family an' friends. This is usually at meal time or every two hours — which ever comes first. We assemble in masses.

We say: 'Let's go get owr gnome boys' (with dramatic flourish) an' we hop, an' we run, an' we climb an' follow his personalized individual gnomal essence scent - an' we track him down in under three days flat (his way of saying a long time.) We all jump with gleeze an' fall on owr rumps an' roll over that we'se all together again. We'se thoughtful an' brought his dinners for him so he can catch up."

"OK. Did you take notes?! (He looks up to the big crowds in the auditorium) Are there any questions? ... OK then! (since no one is answering). Since I've been perfectly succinctable, we can move on to the next lesson."

"Gnome noses get bigga ovah time. This is a sad fact, but it's true. This make owr faces get wider 'cause we have to accommodate it's exceedingly larger proportions. Howevah, an this a very important howevah, the mature gnome nose has a lot of history in it. We'se retain a library of memories an' this is why people say we nose everything."

He's bouncing up and down – and gets a hug.

"Am I an extremely good teacher Daddy?"

"'You are spell-binding," Christian says!

"You are amazing," Christopher exclaims!

Dr. Jacob continues.

"I'm the Gnome, I'm the Gnome!"

"AGRHMMMM!" (He clears his throat.)

"Unbeknowst to humans, gnomes find noses very at-tractive. We think it's one of owr most disting-guish-shading fe-chaws. We can tell what clan you'se come from 'cause your nose is ever so slightly different in size, shape an' ca-lah. Little gnomes always have cute ador-able noses. An' they like to snuggle with 'dem like this (he shows nuzzling.) That's lots like you'se kisses. You'se gnome kids probably snuggle noses with you."

"OK now — I'm ready for my applause. Yes! Yes! I understand the appreciation. But I been to Gnome Uni-versity™ an' I got an' head'ucation! I much brighter than the average gnome 'cause my Daddy has paid my tuition an' sent me out for advanced schooling. I'm learned all 'bout the gnomes so I can be the best doctah when I'm all growed up. But Daddy says don' grow to fast 'cause I'm 'dorable right now."

"I wear a yellow an' white striped smock — 'cause I'm official. An' I gots a big crystal with a hole in it 'round my neck for 'zamning an' healing the hurts. I work well on stomachs an' nervous in-dignation." (Indigestion? This may have more than one meaning.)

He begins clearing his throat: "Urrrhmm, Urgghmm." He puts his hand up to his mouth and whispers:

"It's customary to give the doctah a penny or a dime for his advanced medical treatment programs using only the latest herbal-perfect hypo analgesic non intrusion wholey healt' treatments. Do you want a pamphlet? Be sure an' tell a friend. You should come back twice a week, 'cause you never know when your nerves will act up again."

"Your just a canned ham," Christian says as we both laugh! He laughs. When Jacob first came to us he was extremely shy. We are amazed at the progress he is making.

"Maybe I should do the rest of the book. I got a big vo-carb-alary," he says to laughter.

EEAHS OF EXPERIENCE

Gnomes' ears, or "eah's" as they say, are overall similarly shaped like those of a human's, but with just a little pointyness on the top – though not as long and narrow as elves' ears. The gnome ear offers distinct differences and perhaps advantages over human forms. Appreciating the gnome ears, and hearing, will prove helpful in understanding how the gnomes function in their world, and in ours.

ARE GNOME EARS POINTED

Let's now bring back Dr. Jacob to give us his particularly astute gnome insight. Peter-Jön has indicated that little gnome Dr. Jacob is the designated expert and has the support of our gnome and nature people family to give his dissertation on this subject.

In looking back, as this moment of pride from Dr. Jacob's noble approach to public speaking forces us to do, we remember that Jacob (which is what we originally called him) was rather quiet. Indeed, we recall that we used to have concern over his shyness and his sensitivity to being slightly overweight. He felt he looked somehow different from the other gnomes and wasn't sure how he fit in.

He was exceptional at the time in that he didn't have a

running mate, and gnomes are usually a dual experience. They seem to function as a "set" where each other has different, but complimentary characteristics. Jacob, however, did begin displaying certain intelligence rather early on. He took particularly great concern when there was an illness in the family.

When the gnomes completed the construction of Gnome University™, it was no great surprise that we would soon have a doctor in the family. Indeed, we held great anticipation of just what a gnome doctor would be. We know of their education, as they begin conducting themselves differently.

The way they come across is with what they perceive from their perspectives to be the training and procedures of our professionals whom they model themselves after. They adopt those attitudes and outlooks. To this they blend in the reality of their world. What the gnomes actually experience is different than what humans' would. Therefore, the adaptations better reflect the gnome experience of the roles they are playing. For example, their plumbers may string pipes up and down, sideways and at every conceivable angle, preferring a little whimsy to their design.

"Ahh, here he is." I now step aside as Dr. Jacob makes his authoritative entrance. We can imagine the doors swinging aside as the distinguished doctor briskly enters the room.

> **"It seems you need an expertle opinion on Gnome eaahs."**
>
> — Gnome Dr. Jacob

"Hello Peoples! I's back by exceedingly popular demand. It seems you need an expertle opinion on Gnome eaahs (ears). Well here's the scoop: We'se heah's [hears] good. Owr eaahs can heah sounds that people don' even know exist."

"We heah vibrationally. The things that are 'portant to heah awr vibrational. It tells us when things are healt'y an' working properly. Everything makes sounds. The vibrationals aren' just noise, they got many variations in 'dem that tell us all the character-istics of things."

"We can heah rocks an' trees an' air an' things you don' know exist. When things aren' well they don' sound so good. They vibrate lower an' they sound dull. Very high-pitch, tinggy, small golden bell-sounds are healt'y."

"The gnome eaah canal wraps 'round inside in loops an' this makes the vibrations longer so we can hear 'dem as longer sounds an' can an'lyze 'dem better. Ahh eaahs take apart the sounds, an' we can figure out 'zactly who an' what made 'dem an' what they mean. We'se heah intelligently. Eaahs are the way to go if you really want *to know somethin' smart. We'se don' take shortcuts, we'se listen to everything."*

"If you bounce us around, ah eaahs start ringing inside 'an we can't think clearly, so you gotta play with us nice. Gnomes don't put things in their eaahs like people kids do, 'cause we would just heah those things. Gnomes twist their eaahs sometimes so we can tune out sounds we don't need to be hearing. Don't you wish you could do that? ARGHHHAAaaaa."

"That was a hysterical funny – yes," Christian says.

"Gnomes eaahs are sensitive on top. The tiny, an' I over emphasize tiny, 'pointed' on the top is sensitive to heats an' light. We usually covah are 'pointeds' with owr hats. The 'pointeds' are for fine tuning, 'cause they help us heah those sounds that humans can't heah 'cause the vibrationals are different."

"Humans with big eaahs still can't hear the vibrationals that we heah, 'cause you need to got the whole mechanism made especially for gnomes to heah. 'Sides, humans would't understand the talk'ns that rocks, crystals, an' trees an' watahs make. This is beyond their mental comprehension. That's OK though, u'se guys makes

the best cartoons! An' we can tell what they mean 'cause of the sounds. You use pattern-sounds. OK! I guess I'm talking ovah your head now. I bettah give your brains a break. Don' feel 'timidated by my advanced superiah knowledge. I had to go to school to learn these things."

"We are Eeahs ahead of the Elves"

— Grand Gnome Elder, Wasser-Sisser

"The upper parts of our eeahs can twist ever so slightly from side-to-side, quite elegantly so. Similarly, we can tilt them out and down. Gnomes focus onto sounds through this effective use of our eeahs."

"The elves, however, do no have this exceptional ability. Nonetheless, their remarkable eeahs can tune into the finer sounds of Nature, those not normally heard. They can do so at great distance."

"The elves may hear the distant calls of Nature and point the direction, but it is we gnomes who take in the full nuances of the area around us to find the best path to our destination. We proceed the elves on great journeys to ensure the safest and surest trail."

THE 'DISTINCTABLE' GNOME

Gnomes are "distinctable," they tell us. Their face is round-ish in general. It appears most round in their older age because their nose grows a bit wider and the ears get larger too. Young gnomes don't have beards. As with humans these grow when they reach adulthood. As they get older, their cheeks get puffier, round, and take on a deeper red color. One cannot chance upon a gnome and not notice the purity and eternal youthfulness of their faces. They always look like they are ready to play, laugh or enjoy some great surprise.

The children of the nature people are rather similar to humans, with exception to their size, of course. Yet, their features seem more characteristic, accentuated and expressive. Nature people children will have characteristics of their clans, regions, and groupings too. This means it would not be unusual whatsoever for any of the nature people to have skin coloration which is not our expected flesh tone. Indeed, some nature people are blue, white, green, striped or multicolored. Other variations are distinctive to the environment. For example, desert gnomes and snow gnomes have evolved to naturally take on the coloration of their environments.

Recall, as well, that nature spirits have considerable influence over their appearance as they are essentially Ætheric matter and live partially in the Astral Plane, some even venturing into the Mental Plane. This gives them an intrinsic ability to manifest. The astral crossing is what allows for much of the magic of gnomes. The higher Mental/Heavenly Plane, is where the High Magic and miracles are performed by leprechauns, salamanders, and cloud spirits.

The current physical environment may suggest to gnomes that certain sizes, characteristics, clothing and appearance would be most appropriate. When they adopt a human family they will try to fit in with the looks that human children have. You might routinely see them running around in white Jedi® robes, Superman® and Flash® costumes, pampers®, and cargo shorts. They will dress up in their rendition of swim-wear for your pool parties and don formal attire (shorts, shirt, tie and highly polished shoes) for evenings out, special occasions, and when company arrives.

Now we want to emphasize their creative interpretations. By way of illustration, the Superman® costumes they make might have an emblazoned "G" instead of an "S". When they play Star Wars®, everyone is the good guy (there are no bad guys) and their light sabers are like flashlights. They have no concept of hurting each other.

They can also be consistent with their imagery. If they're watching *Star Trek*®, they wear an insignia badge on their uniforms. If an old Errol Flynn movie is on television, like *Robin Hood* for example, they can be seen traipsing around with pointed elf hats sporting long pheasant feathers. Not all of their attire is a manifestation. The clans have women that are skilled seamstresses and they readily replicate their version of human play-clothes, costumes, and formal attire. These are actually "real," albeit of Ætheric matter.

When there are no longer reasons to maintain the manifestations of size or appearance, they simply return to their natural state as this does not require an extra expenditure of energy.

Gnome Rudabegah

Rudabegah is one of the latter arrivals to the family. He is from the mountain clan. Rudabegah is tall and lean, which is not the conventional build of gnomes. He also has a head of bushy hair which is cute on a child but would drive a barber to the limits of his passion. For now, all the reddish-golden locks stay and we turn over the topic of Gnome Features to Rudabegah to expound upon.

> **"Peoples can't see us'es gnomes all the time."**
> — Gnome Rudabegah

"'Cause I's the newest I's knows best'est the things that the new gnomes do."

"He's also got a little friend with him, Curly Cue. Perhaps together they can give us more insight on gnome attire and manifestation, or characteristics ... should they desire," Christian says.

GNOMES LIKE TEDDY BEARS

"Peoples can't see us'es gnomes all the time. But they feel us an' heah [hear] us quite a bunch. The first gnomes in the family came up with an idea. They saw lots an' lots of people's children with stuffy bears, anumals an' dolls. You can use these to pretend they're us so we feel more hard to you all the time."

"But, you got to let us pick out owr own stuffy or doll. The character-istics you feel 'bout us will tell you to make the right pick. For zample people: If I had big eahs, [ears] which I don' by the way, you will feel related [drawn] to a stuffy bear with big eahs! If I have lots of curly hair, then you might see one with curly hair that is like me'se that you like. You will also be mez-merized to

get the right hair color. Hahahah."

"Then you can squeeze us an' kiss us an' hug us, an' take us for rides, an' put us to bed at about four (4:00 PM) for owr naps. This is helpful until those times you see us for real! An' also those times when were not easily visible during the day - 'cause of the bad lighting conditions."

"When we go sleepies we crawl into the stuffy bear so you can lift us up and say: 'night, night!' An' you can put us to sleep on the pillows. At Christmastime you can put us in the stock'ns or in the Christmas tree. We aren' really the bears, or anumals or dolls, we just get in 'dem so we feel more real to you and you treat us for real."

"If you buy us'es at the store, you want to take off the ribbons an' things so you can put clothes on us. 'Cause we like getting dressed up like real people children do. We took off my brown ribbon today an' put on a white 'onesie' (one-piece found in 1-6 month baby clothing section.) We used the brown ribbon to tie 'round the ways [waist] an' today I get to be a Jedi Knight® or a karate kid! (he lifts his foot and saying KAWAOW!) Most 'portant, you got to take the stickers off owr bottoms so they don' send us back to China. KAOW! CHEW! (Kick-

ing legs.)"

"You want to get the bears that have the right eyes an' face that you are feeling an' seeing inside. This will help you — little people, when you try an' talk to us. We will usually tell you things, ... just before you think to ask. But, you will know it's com'n from us 'cause the things that we tell you will all come true."

"Wow!" we both say in unison.

We find their premonitions occur more than 8 hours later, and usually closer to 24.

Curly Cue

Little Curly Cue is gnome Rudabegah's closest friend. He is going to talk about his teddy bear. He mysteriously has a pink quartz crystals in his hand again! Every time Christian goes to pick him up he seems to have these crystals.

"I's a soccer star!"

— Gnome Curley Cue

"Today I got on little baby stock'ns from the K-Mart store (actually Wal-Mart but Chris always accidentally calls them K-Mart). I got soccer balls on my stock'ns (baby socks). My stock'ns are wayze too big for me — but

I love 'em! An' they covah my whole leg'ees. An' every-
one knows I'm a soccer-star — (and then the crystal fell
in front of his feet!) My name is Curly Cue 'an my stuffy-
bear has short curly hair. I like to go outside an' play a
lot. But 'cause I get so dirty bee'in a super soccer star an'
all, I have to leave my bear inside. 'Else I have to take a
bath every night. Them'se the rules."

"We have little people dolls too — in the gnome vil-
lages. They'se look just like you. We put the little people
dolls on owr pillows when we sleep in owr gnome beds.
That way the peoples can be with us too. (He's playing
with his crystal soccer ball, kicking it.) We like the toys
that the peoples give us. Like the little 'cahs, an' the
tractors, an' fiyah-engines, an' the buses, an' the choo
choo trains. The girls use the little sewing machine every
day."

THE RE-APPEARING ACT
Christian

"Curly Cue suddenly has two crystals in front of him,"
Christian exclaims to Chris!   "Are you doing magic tricks,"
Christian asks Curly Cue?

"One for you one for me," he says.

Christian thanks him as Christopher sees the small crystal

balls in similar amazement.

Christopher

"Now the fairy "Tinkles," also known as Tinkle Bear, wants to jump in. We should inform you that Tinkles isn't a gnome, but rather, a fairy. He picked out his own teddy bear – although it took him about two weeks before he and I found the right one together. This was a little four-inch bear that has a great big red three-musketeer type hat on it with a rose stitched to one side. It also has a pearl necklace, and a royal purple cape. There is, in addition to the already mentioned wardrobe, a lavender and white gossamer ribbon wrapped around the hat. This prize bear now sports a skirt of many gossamer petals with sparkly flowers on the tips."

Fairy Tinkle Bear

> *"I'm the newest!!!"*
>
> — Fairy Tinkles

The nature spirit family might say that they are the newest throughout the book, which is true. Keep in mind it was written over the course of many years.

> *"What ahh you doin' theah?! The thocks [socks] are twos big, I can't stand up! My thocks ahh twos big for this bear. The knuckles are on top. How come is that?"*

Christopher stops to fix it.

> *"I'm's an Appalachian Tree Fairy. And I probably wouldn't be here if it wasn't convenient! 'Cause you'se are in the mountains, I guess I can play with the family every day."*

Fairies seem to have lots of attitude. We think that this may simply be that they are somewhat literal, and it is we humans who place our connotations on their words.

> *"We'se fairies are fussy. We like things awr way — So you bettah know that!"*

Christopher and Christian start talking about Smurrf, their Blue Faerie, trying to compare the two.

> *"Hey, I'm talking to you! Are you Mormon or something? We like things clean and nature fresh. Them's the rules! You guys have to pick aftah your trash. We don't throw our stuff in your yard. We do like to keep our trees clean an' healthy, though. So, it's OK to clean the messy branches on the bottoms off."*

> *"I'm a little tike but I got 'bilities. I make the trees smell really good. Trees smell is 'portant 'cause it 'tracts the right birds. An' the birds knock down the pine cones*

an' new trees can grow. There are lots of fairies out there in the world, all different bunches of kinds. An' lots an' lots of people can see fairies. Do you peoples know that we're 'spose to wave when we see humans? We know the good humans — 'cause they're the one's that wave back."

"We like lots of colors an' brightness. Sometimes you see us as lights or twinkling but if you unfuse your eyes more you'll see we look like little people too'se [pronounced tooz]. Fairies look a lot like people — only much bettah look'n. We don't do the manifesting as much as the gnomes, an' I know we're 'spose to talk about that, but we talk a lot. We talk an' we talk an' we talk an' we talk. When you see us, we is usually in a group talking or singing or making beautiful things. We'll talk to you too — but you gottah keep up. 'Cause we'se fairies is reeal smart."

THESE ARE PARTING WORDS
"Where they's Birds, fairies will soon follow."

That is why, we have been told by the fairies, that putting out seeds for the birds is a good thing because you also will be attracting fairies. "Thank you Tinkles," Christopher says.

HATS ARE THEIR TRADE

Gnomes are universally recognized by their hats. Tradition shows them in a round pointed cone-shaped cap. These vary somewhat in the depictions - - red or green, perhaps flopping over at the top, some firm, some soft. In reality there is a specific shape to the gnome hat. It is a straight and conical pointed cap. There are, however, nuances so subtle to the human eye that they are missed. These have significant meaning to other gnomes and even other nature people.

Gnomes can recognize the clan that another is from just by the shading of red, green or pertinent color. Height and stiffness signify relevant information. The hat is a beacon. It is a banner and a trademark. As such, it signals their age, skills and status. Even a certain wrinkle, ever so slight, may yield valuable clues about the neighborhood the gnome belongs too.

Occasions may warrant specific attire as well, be they formal, functional or vocational. Ceremonies may find the gnomes in hats that are adorned using some relevant component of nature. For example: The clan leader may rope fine gold twine around a highly polished conical black hat, and add a tassel, flower or shaft of wheat for ceremonies such as seasonal holidays or weddings. Feathers, pine cones, berries, clovers or significant ornamentation may be worn when meeting the leaders of another kingdom. We have observed this on occasions where they met contingents from the Elfin Kingdom.

The children may manifest all manners of fanciful hats and attire to supplement their playtime imaginings. Imagination is an important part of all of their activities. As indicated previously, external influences such as television, neighborhood parties and family events find them gleefully romping and playing as pretend super-heroes and colorful characters. They manifest reasonably accurate attire, including hats, as befits the occasion.

Our nature people family is most apt to coordinate their couture to match family festivities. Peter-Jön, our first gnome and nature spirit in the family, surprised us one day with the most colorful pool-side swimwear, shortly after asking us if he could have a barbeque and swimming party for the neighborhood [nature people] kids and adults.

"Hats make the man"

— Grand Gnome Elder, Wasser-Sissor

"Our hats are an important part of our lives as they communicate identity, trade, status and rank."

PETER-JöN MAKES A SPLASH

When Peter-Jön got the OK for his pool party he was dressed in a flash and a flourish. The barbeque was rolled out and the pool abounded in air toys. This was HIS first "to-do" for the clan. It was only fitting that he should be sporting an appropriate pool hat to set the tone. This one is *not* in their record books.

"We weah happy cloths!"

— Gnome Peter-Jön

"UMPH! It is as simple as that. If it makes us happy, then we make the clotheses poof out from our mind. This takes considerable, specialized, often qualified skill. I am exceedingly specialized in this task — 'cause I watch the most cartoons of anybody. Cartoons show us how to do everything."

"That's how we know how to crawl up to the birds without them flying away. They we'rnt sus-pish-alized by us when twenty-four secret agent gnomes with reeds an' furry grass in our caps sneaked up and counted all their eggs. We shouldn't have touched any though, 'cause theah eahrs still heard us. We had to go back the next day an' do it allh ovah again, but this time we put duck feathers on ourah mittens. This took much longah. But they weren't sus-pish-ialized."

"Everette had to count the burds an' figah out where everyone of them was flying too, 'cause the school made him do it. They said we'se all 'spose to know what the burds do. We can't take theah eggs when it's special sea-son 'cause the new burds have to get started out. But we can take their nesting weeds an' make yummy soups.

Sometimes we have to weah camel-flogged pants-es too or the fishes will give us away. We tied leaves to our pants-es and they didn't even know. Hahhahaaaahhh. We smartah then fishes."

"Gnomes, 'escuse me, kids gnomes, like to weare different bright colahs. This is so we can tell each othah apart. Othah wise, we'se all just look adorable. AGHahhhhhh! We use the colahs so we can play the different people (characters in a game). White is for the goodest people, but our favorite colahs are red and gween and blue and yellow and marshmallow aaaannnnn' berry, an' bubblegum. We pick the colahs too. It works for us. We each have colahs that are awrs. Mine's red, and everybody knows it."

Christopher asks for any extra information relating to the standard hat color and nuances that yield valuable information to gnomes and the rest of the Nature Spirit kingdom.

"You have it all extorted. We has pretty colahs too. We likes yellow, an' almost a hundred shades of blue, an' maybe three hundred shades of gween, an' purpah is for very impo-tant people. We'se got orange, but that's mostly for the mommies, and they like buttah colors too, and

creamy ones. *Dark brown an' dark gween an' dark blue are for workers. They indicate groundwork, flower work, an' high-sky (smart) work. That's pretty simple isn't it Christopha?"*

"The white hats can only be worn by the spirit-wizards, an' I don' know if I can talk 'bout dem, but their hats sparkle some. I think they buy dem at Disneyland® 'cause they look like they been papered with fairy wings. Only the spirit-wizards can tie colored ribbons around their hats 'cause that's magical. An' I don' know if I can talk about dem. The spirit wizards have long gold sticks with light [like actual lights] rocks on the top, an' I don' know if I can talk about that. We don' have witches hats, 'cause we don' have witches 'cause nobodies ugly and we have beautiful noses!"

Christopher asks, "Do the wrinkles on the hat mean something or is the location important?"

"We don' iyon [iron] very much so they get wrinkles. But maybe you mean folds? Dem's like notches to indicate higher-ups. But also angles of the folds mean more sometimes. Like you guys use costumes for the North an' for the Southern peoples, we fold them differently. This is 'cause we have more directions than you peoples do."

"We can say peoples (nature-peoples) come from any direction but we can also say how high they are, like in the mountains - like from the Northern flatlands, or the Northern valley, or the Northern mountains. When the tip-top is folded ovah it in-di-cators these gnomes be by watah too. This usually means there's big 'campments, food for travelers, an' places to stay. Fah-mahs put leaves an' cones an' wheats, an' things in their gween hats to in-di-cators what they'se fah-men. Do you'se want to talk about the fish-a-mens too? AGhhhhhh. [He's teezing Chris.] Elfs bring most of the fishes an' we trade with dem. They just show up un-'nounced 'cause their real quiet."

"Gnomes aren't allowed to wear bells in dah hats for real gnome stuff. That's for people play time. We can heah the bells on those times. (He is talking about Christmas hats.) The bells sound wrong though an' they all need to be fixed. But that's the fairies' jobs."

"Christopha we don' always wear pointy hats. Pointy hats are for when your travel'n places an' people have to see you. We weah the floppy kind when were playin at home an' stuff. I hope I'n not ruin' you book?"

"We do weah caps or hats most of the time cause owrs

hairs is long an' gets caught in the bushes an' trees. Also, it's 'portant sometimes to covah the tips of dah eahs cause the noise can be distracting.   If owr eahs are dirty the hats covah them up an' we don't have to go up the creek. We don't like go'n into the creek all the time. Brrrrrhhhhh. (Christopher wants to know if they keep things in their hat.) OK, Christophah! I wasn't gonna tell you but I will. We use our big hats for carrying stuff too. We put lots of things in da hats that we might need when we'se walk'n 'round. They'se like knapsacks. But mostly we put sleepy stuff in dar, an' other clotheses. Do you wanta grill me some more?"

 "Do younger gnomes have longer hats or shorter? Do they get stiffer hats as they get more status or position in life," Christopher asks?

"Daddy, he's like the Bat-man (They think of this as bad man) show — there's the light (points to table lamp) …. He's gong to tie me to the chair too -- no no I'm not gonna talk. Daddy, he doesn't know anything. Should I tell him — or should it be our little secret?"

Christian tells him he can tell Christopher some stuff. "You don't have to tell me either, or you can keep it a secret if you want."

"OK mistah Bat-man I only got three minutes to 'phes up or its KOWEY (K-POW!) The littah one's always wear liiittah cap hats that are softie. 'Cause they ain' nobody, an' everybody already knows the little kids. If they wore stiff hats, they would just come off, but anyway they don' need stiff hats 'cause they ain' travel'n. Stiff hats are watah proof. So little kids aren' gonna be walk'n any-where in the rain. Sheeesh! They can have stiff hats when they old enough to travel without someone hold'n dem."

Christopher

I thank Peter-Jön over and over for explaining to us so much about gnome hats – possibly one of their most recognized characteristics, one known around the world.

The neighborhood nature people can be seen properly equipped and suited to carry on important developmental activities. One such activity of recent note is their jaunts to the nearby duck preserve to silently observe the comings and goings of the seasonal sojourns as well as local nesting habits. They don camouflaged hats of green and brown with tall grass attached to them. Such hats are quite charming but serve a purpose in making them invisible to ducks and wildlife when they go bird watching.

The Elves tend to be in style.

— Peabody, Leprechaun Elder/Leader

Elder Peabody is a Leprechaun. Nonetheless, diplomats as they all are, he is going to share some insight on Elf hats.

"Elves wear more fashion oriented headwear, and it is often adorned, don't you know? Now, their hats do not so plainly distinguish them as they may choose to wear none at'all. When they do, mind you, there are some distinguishing characteristics."

"First, being civilized folk, they tend to have some form of brim, even if it is slight. The more labor situated elves have brims or bands that can also hold small papers. These may be codified maps or elfin papers of introduction. Green is their color of choice, and a fine color it is. They blend into their environment better that way. Styles can express their trade or location."

"Adornment of jewels and crystals is likely, and metals too; the more notable, the more bejeweled. Like all good kings, their leaders will wear more adornment, although the style is light and tasteful."

ෆ PART – II ෨

THE GREAT GNOME
KINGDOMS

GNOME REGIONS AND TERRITORIES

The diversity of gnomes is expressed in Great Regions and Territories. The divisions within these vary by continent in respect to name. These may be similar to area-names used currently, but not necessarily. Geography always is a factor, as collectively, all territories and regions have a practical significance.

Throughout North America a division of States is used, however, the term Province is not. Note that these gnome boundaries do not correlate with those of the American States. Although geographic, the boundaries represent a contained area that also has a descriptive purpose, function or orientation.

CLANS

Within any State there will be an individual Kingdom with a composition of Townships, Villages and Hobbles. Hobbles are a clustering of dwellings. These are a geographic organization of the Gnome peoples. Overlaying these Townships, Villages and Hobbles are Clans, which are divisions, based upon both local cultures, and convenience, not geography

THE LANDS

Any area within North America can also be referred to generically as "lands." In Europe, however, "lands" would be a specific term analogous to States as described above, and Individual Kingdoms would be in these lands. Further, within these can be constabularies, and then villages and hobbles. Constabulary does not refer to a police territory as commonly used by humans. Although not generally used any more, there use to be comparable divisions within the Individual Kingdoms referred to as Vales and Encampments.

In South America the area descriptions are fewer because fewer gnomes are associated with a particular grouping. This would be true for Mexico through Central America as well. In other words, individual kingdoms can be extremely vast. Organizationally, there are fewer differences that would necessitate smaller divisions. Eurasia and the Balkans use the terms lands, courts, villages and "places," after translation.

Individual kingdoms are not established as political seats of power. These are built around commerce and communication hubs. It is the "kingdom" that is significant over "the Leader" of an individual kingdom.

GHOB WATCHES OVA'H US

THERE IS ONE LEADER OVER EARTH

Besides having the wise counsel of the elders of the clan, who may individually be easily thousands of years old, the gnomes across the globe do have one central leader, Ghob.

Ghob is actually the High King of not only the Gnomes, but also of the entire Earth Nature Spirit Kingdom. He is much taller than the typical gnome, about four and a half feet in height. He distinctively has wiry hair and a usually serious look to match his demeanor. He appears fierce and this might cause pause for any human who chances upon him. Ghob takes his role as their leader, and more importantly, their protector, quite seriously.

He is usually sighted at gatherings or locales where protection is warranted or there is a transition of control from one nature spirit type to another. Ghob will oversee such matters to ensure there is peace and harmony between these disparate groups. He also oversees the establishment of the physical location of a new clan. He can often be seen on guard for several days to establish his acceptance and dominion. His appearance is a tacit stamp of approval.

He has a purpose in life of TOTAL responsibility.

— Ghob has indicated

A BRIEF DISCUSSION WITH GHOB

Christian
He tells us that he is the only Nature Spirit that can appear in more than one location at the same time.

HE CAN SHAKE THE WORLD
Such information from Ghob is amazing since we had never heard him speak to the world of humans in text before. Whereas gnomes exhibit a sense of playfulness and serenity, even in their work, Ghob reflects a counterpart of collective responsibility for all gnomes.

Although he is in essence the responsible one, we have seen him smile and joke on rare occasion and even show a slight humanizing trait of personality. He once asked if his hair was OK, at a time when we were trying to spiff up the clan for some celebratory event. In showing us a type of vulnerability, we found him more approachable and real as a person. He says his moments of levity are few and far between, and even then would normally have to follow some job well done.

Ghob will delegate to great legions certain responsibilities once his control over a matter has been established. He is then free to communicate and interact on a more personable level. When Ghob speaks, nothing is allowed to be written down. So, great care and effort is put into his words, his actions, and the understanding of these by the nature people.

He communicates in a way that is experiential so that everyone gains the full import and impact of his messages and intents. The gnomes and nature people do not bow down and grovel when before him. However, they demonstrate their highest level of respect, conduct, and attitude while in his presence.

GHOB ESCHEWS POMP AND CEREMONY

Ghob arrives unannounced eschewing all pomp and ceremony as might be typical of clan leaders. That he can arrive unceremoniously is cause for much of the respect attributed for him. He is not there to be idolized or adored, he is there to be understood, and this is clear to all nature spirits of the Earth. He is thought to be a direct channel for Archangel Uriel. And the gnomes have no doubt about this. Ghob is never questioned.

THE GNOMES HAVE WARRIOR PROTECTORS

The gnomes have warrior protectors who have a much different look than typical nature people, and are more akin to Ghob. They are taller and leaner than the gnome. They carry a long rod or staff and possibly a spear with them. They are called in or arrive when the clan may need protection of their newfound wealth. Such may be may be mounds of rich dirt added to their surroundings. The warriors may arrive for the protection of the gnomes. They also protect humans who are on spiritual quests. The gnomes know these protectors as part of a group called "the Caretakers".

GNOME CLANS

CULTURAL GROUPINGS

Clans are "cultural" groupings that can exist in or about most of the gnome-peopled areas already described. However, they will always be smaller than a Territory. Clans have "functional" borders based on responsibility and may or may not reflect the physical borders of any individual community. Not everyone in the clan is from the same family name, or originates from the same locale, or has similar monetary status. Gnome clans are comprised of families of varied heritage (country of origin, family names and status.)

COMMUNITY

Gnomes work together quite well in community-like endeavors. They have group elders who make important decisions that will govern the clan, and interaction among people.

Gnomes get along amazingly well, whether with those of their clan or with other clans worldwide. They identify with the phylum, not the geography. Their sense of community within the clan is admirable too. They all work together for the common good and rarely, if ever, seem to argue amongst themselves. Watching gnomes in an argument is like watching those battles where men dress up in those blow-up sumo-wrestler size suites. It's almost impossible to have anger, but rather, everything is a reason to laugh together.

Should a serious issue arise that needs to be sorted-out between gnome families, then one elder or a small council of elders WILL resolve the matter, and that will be that. Wisdom, reason and experience will prevail. The elders draw from countless centuries of precedence in all matters. Elders from different clans may communicate with each other directly should there be an issue involving individuals or families of different clans.

GNOME LANGUAGE

Do gnomes specifically use their own language for important topics or for profound talks? This is one of the first interview questions we had with Charles.

Speaking about gnome language

— Gnome Expert Charles

"Nature peoples 'dopt the language of the environment they lives in. It must be 'cepted, that wheres local languages are used the nature peoples will have the interpretation of the meaning of things — an' only some things. It should not be pre-zzz-umed that all the words an' all the nuances are understood, or understood well."

"The nature peoples takes general understanding of those things an' add a meaning that they commonly understand to those words, [phrases, actions, or customs.] So, we do have a way of trans-1-ating from our culture to yours, and to various regions of the world. It is a hard thing to understand when you realize that the nature people kingdoms existed, or have existed, far, far, far in excess of most of the [human] cultures of the day. And for such excess time we have been able to make these trans-

l-ations."

The gnomes have also a base-language, which can vary from region to region, but not so much. It would be true that this base-language remains generally constant around the world, or at least the greater parts of the world. Gnome Chester (one of our astute child gnomes) indicates that the base-language must be used where man is not indigenous. There are also certain ceremonies that do not have a human counterpart. In such cases the gnome base-language would be used.

There are values that the gnomes carry across generations ... across peoples, and across lands. The base-language will relate to these traditions. There are some habitual facets of their lives that have to do with trading, and which have components that are transacted and discussed in their base-language. Unlike humans, gnomes do not have a problem of mixing these two forms.

In environments where intercommunication among different nature spirit types is prevalent, it is similarly necessary that they intercommunicate in their base-languages. In this instance, the better known meanings and expressions are familiar and adaptation is not necessary.

Gnome Charles has indicated that there is much of human culture that the gnomes simply consider nonsense, in which case they are dismissive of it ... as it pertains to humans. For example, a lot of what humans will say, the gnomes will simply ignore. Similarly, much of what humans do will be disregarded. Furthermore, the way humans appear, and that which they believe in, will be overlooked.

GNOME CUSTOMS

It is important that the nature people maintain certain customs. These transcend the times, the regions and locations. There are customs that remain consistent and are very highly respected. These need to be carried out in certain ways, time after time. For example: the gnomes expect remuneration for goods or services. Things are [traded] not just given.

Over the years we have learned that gnomes will give freely if a fellow nature person is in need of food – even if he has nothing to trade in return. Their system of trade is not as demanding as you will see in subsequent paragraphs. They deem trading more as "sharing". Sharing something another gnome, elf, leprechaun or fairy has need of, in return for the same consideration.

GNOME SPIRITUALITY

The gnomes are open to our human beliefs. This does not preclude them from maintaining reverence for their own spiritual viewpoint, which may be considered religious. Indeed, they do have their own connection to spirit; they have ceremonies, and religious customs.

In essence, they incorporate the religions of their hosting families and environments into their way of life. Gnome spirituality is a connection to higher realms of consciousness, and does not so much require the formality of human religions since it is rather an individual experience, although shared collectively. They see Angels, Archangels and other High forms of consciousness, as they have expressed this to us. As a family, we have collectively experienced angels, Archangels, deities and Ascended Masters.

"We have ancient beliefs"

—— Gnome Peter-Jön tells us

"We'se the gnomes don't make up new beliefs. We'se use the same one's we always did - 'cause if they were true in the beginning, they must be true now. Owr beliefs awr acknowledgments of the Great Spirits of things an' of the workings of the world. There's nothing that evah changes. So every one of the gnomes, and ac-tu-aly

most nature people, have the same feelings about things an' the same reverence for the Angel people, an' for the Spirits, an' for the Energy, an' even for owr way of life."

"This is why all the nature people respect Ghob, 'cause Ghob has been Ghob to everybody. An' we actually get to see him sometimes. There are some othah great leaders too, 'cause of the different kind of nature people. Since the'se real, they just tell us the stories every so often so we all have the same knowledge. We don't all always understand it as well as some othahs, but we know to follow the same routines an' the same methods as owr fellows, which is how you church people call brothers, 'cause we know with complete certainty that when we're done getting biggah, everthing will make complete sense."

"All the gnomes have to do is work hard, always keep their jobs, an' live in happiness an' harmony to the most possible. An' everything will work out the way it's 'spose too. We don't have to pressah [pressure] our minds like the humans do. Even though owrs awr softah, we don't do this. But the big peoples get the headaches 'cause the every peoples [everyone] havn't got things figured out yet. 'Cause they'se so tall, it must take much longah for the knowledge to reach their brains. An' 'cause they'se hard-headed an' not softies, most of it can't get in any-way."

"We'se don't understand why they havn't figured everything out yet. Or just take the wurds from the Great Spirits who are always there, an' write them down once an' for all — so it's done with."

"What the peoples keep believ-ens in an' fighten about isn't the things that the Big Spirits are say'in anyway. There's noth'in to have upsets ovah in what They'se sayin'. How's can you fight ovah having to love everybody an' everything, which is something you don't understand at all yet? Your big guys [Archangels, Ascended Masters, etc.] say, "All of the world is something to love.""

"What we'se been seein' goin' on — an' this is from our 'rspective, which is much shorter than yours — is that there's nothing knew to learn in the world. You'se just have to look around an' see how the trees, an' the rocks, an' the animals have worked it out. You gots to do the same things — an' then you'll be in hamony [harmony] with each other an' everything. You don't need to be a brain scientist to get this. Everything 'is' an' that's just the way it's gonna be. So what do you wanna do about it?"

"*Every peoples an' everything has to live to the highest level of their greatest happiness. That means everybody an' everything will love equally, everybody an' everything. Then the whole world lives togethah like a great big family. That's why we'se here's talking to you in the books. We'se currently really big on helping the human peoples understands family from the world perspective. Is that the right word Daddy? 'Yes, that's the right word [perspective] — that makes sense.' You'se really just big gnomes with attitude. (we laugh) You gottah stop eating all the sour grapes. We'll show you where the good stuff is.*"

"*We have anothah perspective — if we may? It seems to us that the big people always have the thoughts about themselves. That isn't the way the rest of the world thinks. All the rocks want to be sure that the othah rocks are doin' well. Each tree wants to be sure that all the othahs in the flock are getting sunshine an' watah too, an' the gnomes an' the othah guys wants to be sure everyone has someone to play with. There's gottah be someone that's perfect for everyone out therah. So everybody can be happy as the next guy — an' have all the same enjoyments in life. It's really very simple from owr little points of view.*"

"We'se look at all the new people we can share things with when we come across othah gnomes or elves on our journeys. Humans say 'Oh no! — there's not enough to go around,' but there's always enough love an' happiness inside you stuffed in the areas where you nevah go to share with everyone you meet. So just give a little from those areas inside of you that you nevah visit. An' you won't have lost anything. The uddah guys [the people you give it too] are gonna replace it right away anyway. This is why we call it sharing — an' not giving up."

GNOME CULTURE

LIVE LONG AND PROSPER

Gnomes benefit from an individual longevity and a collective existence that exceeds our sense of the ages, and is almost beyond our comprehension. Their culture is steeped in time-honored tradition, and "proven" methods which add richness and harmony to their lives.

"We'se live longah 'cause we're happier people."

— Peter-Jön says:

"There's too much wonderment in the world to give up on right away. We've barely got through the playing stages an' hope we don't have to stop that anytime soon. Here's the real deal you big peoples, there's a great big bunch dat we have to learn in the world. It comes slowly. So we'se got to stick around 'till we learn a few things. But we'se willing to stick around."

"The humans are always 'spectin it to end any day now. Why is dat? Don' you want to stick sround for the big party? Owr filosophies awr that 'if you're having fun being a little boy or girl — then enjoy it!' Make all *the friends that you can. If you trade marbles with all the gnomes, then one day you'll have a big collection. An' the more friends you have, the more things your gonna learn. But dat's gonna be the fun stuff in life dat you ALWAYS remember. So you don' wanna rush the child-hood, 'cause dat's the biggest part of life. With the gnomes peoples we'se allowed to be childhoods as long as we want to be. An' let me assures you — dat's a very long time. There's no sense in loosing all your marbles too early on."*

"We'se all got togethah an' thought about this long an' hard. An' calculated that we live longah 'cause we'se happier. We'se look forward to each new day. Happiness makes us healthier. We'se not sick of tomorrow. So's all you'se people have to do is live like little gnomes, collect your marbles, an' be healthy an' you too can live long an' prosper."

"Gnomes all live to be three to four hundred thou-sands of years old — at least. We'se have classes of gnomes based on our intelligence an' heritage. Some of these classes can be fourteen thousand thousands years old. There are some exceptions dat live to be forty thousand thousands years old."

"*Owr old people don' loose their faculties like the humans, 'cause they live good lives. They become wise instead. An' they know everything there is to know in the world. So we look up to owr old people with admiration 'cause they'se mystical an' magical an' can teach us great things.*"

"*All the gramps an' grannies can do things to bedazzle us 'cause they'se lived long enough to learn all the tricks in life. They tell us — 'The biggest secret of all is to find out who you are, an' be the best gnome that you can be!'*"

"*That's why the gnomes are so eagah to have a job. So's they can start being the best at it. We awr very happy with owr jobs 'cause it's special, just for us. It doesn't matter to each-uthah what we do, it matters that we have a purpose. So's we very happy mak'in hats or fix'n pipes or huntin' down ducks for bird nest soup 'cause we'se going to be the very best at it.*"

"*Then all the magic in life comes easy, 'cause we'se got nothing to worry about. When you've got sumpin' that you'se good at, you'se gonna be happy. An' everybody 'round, from all the kingdoms even, are gonna know if you'se a tinkah [tinker] — you'se a darn good tinkah.*

Not just a little tinkah [stinker] — hahhah."

"The happier we'se be, an' the more fulfilled we awr 'cause we have jobs, the longah we live an' the more time we have to learn all the secrets of the forest. That's how you become magical like Granny. Grannies talk with all the other grannies from the fairies an' the elves, an' they trade secrets in their recipe books. An' this makes them happieh, 'cause they can take care of the little 'uns bettah."

SLOW CHANGING CULTURE

Gnome culture evolves more slowly than ours as the influences in their lives are not as fast changing as with humans. Change has affected the gnome peoples, however, and this is partially the reason that there is more contact and connection between the Nature Spirit world, and ours currently. To better understand the gnomes it is necessary to take a look at their culture and society. There are elements of it which must be respected as a "working" means to their lives. Our respect will help us co-exist more harmoniously.

SOCIETAL STRUCTURE

SIMPLISTIC

The gnomes do not have an overly structured hierarchical society. It is based on their peoples and not on politics, dogma, backgrounds or beliefs. Society provides the means for the collective of individuals to come together for common functions, purposes and benefits. It provides yet another way in which the gnomes share. They share of themselves with each other and they share their individuality and celebrate it in each other.

INDIVIDUALITY

As individuals, each gnome has his or her own proclivity. Unlike humans, these proclivities can actually be generational traits. Their choices are not so much democratic as they are genetic. For example, a child may be born to be a miner, a carpenter, a seamstress, baker, cheese-jerker [cheese maker], or a shop keeper; it is in his or her makeup.

Gnome families can be naturally oriented towards specific professions and interests. The gnome clans allow for the individual and families to follow their personal direction and rather sensibly incorporate such inclination in a way that benefits the entire clan. Gnomes enjoy a "natural" harmony as they individually, as families and as a clan follow their own natural direction.

"I'm a singer, but I can also do ac-counting."

— Gnome Chester says

"Since I'm multi-tudin'l I's get to pursue both. When gnomes'es kids have more than one 'drawing' [calling] they are good candidates for being part of a human family where their 'bilities can be better dev'loped. So, this is a clue. If you have gnomes in your family, these [gnomes] are probably verrrry talented." (Chester is also the map-maker and keeper, the leader of the children when they are in groups, the chef and an example of sophisticated culture.)

"I's allowed to pursue anythings that I's wants too. An' here's the deal on that: Normally we'se one thing for a long time. Then when we become overdev'loped, we have some new interests, an' we'se allowed to do that. Recently, since we've been including short term humans in owr lives, we've been able to do more things an' new things more quickly so we can make owr families happier. But in the end, most gnomes dev'lop skills in almost all areas during their lifetime."

"There is one difference. An' that has to do with talent. Talent is a unique 'bility. For example: I'm probably the greatest singah in the known world. Who would

have guessed?! That's 'cause I's got talents for it. Peter-Jön can only sing to rocks. Hahahaa. Or at least that's all who listen to him. But I's can sing to the trees. An' they join in with their beautiful chorus; an' we make the whole forest come alive with music."

"So you see, I'm pretty exceptional. PJ does have that mental gift though. I guess we have to give him that one though. These drawings [callings] are the real featcha [feature] they will try an' bring out in the families an' groupings. The others are like playtime."

"Also 'portant is that differen' gnomes have differen' 'telligences. That's why I's a natural ac-countant. 'Cause I can figah out anything that has more than one numbah in it. I'm up to my three's now — so nothin' get's past me. Not every gnome can do this kind of 'vanced calc-a-lating. So I'm rather rare. But I'm well done too!" (Ohh My goodness — a pun!)

"It's seems to me that all gnomes are actors. I've nevah met one that didn't want to be a this - or a that. That's why we like the super costumes an' the cowboys an' being all the characters we can be — sometimes birds. Actin' the birds is harder 'cause we have to fly. We'se actors like to be like you in you'wr jobs too. So we'se *learn how to do all sorts of things. Like driving buses, an' making the forks lift; an' makin' the hairs turn different colahs, an' floppin' the pizzas."*

"Gnomes love to act as the waiters an' the cookers. That's really fun for all of us. You see us at every of you'wr restaurants bringing you the coffees an' the burnt toast. 'Sorry 'bout that. It wasn't burnt when we put it in.' But we'se really good at being waiters an' we'se like all the pennies an' coins that you leave us on the tables for doin' such a good acting job. We'se always take a bow before we'se accept the coins and send you happyily on your ways after our stupendous serving performance. You usually leave very pleased, as long as we'se fast with the grub."

"All the big gnomes have jobs too. Only they'se not acting so much. They'se are really serious doormen an' mailmen. An' they'se always on duty. They'se are the one's you hear say'in 'Good Day Ma'm!' in the back of your head. An', 'My, you sure look lovely today!' They've learned all the fine things to say to make your day brighter."

"You should look for them out of the corner of your eye. Those times you are wishing someone would say nice

things to you, are really thoughts of you knowing we gnomes already awr. So say 'Thank you' back for owr politness, an' we'll keep being nice to you. That will put a smile on your face."

"If you think about it for just a moment, you will even catch owr name. It will be right on the tip of you'wr mind. Say, 'Thank you very much Pierre!' an' we will say, 'Ohhh no no Maimseille, it is I who am so pleased at your radiance. Please let me get the door for you. What a lovely smile you'wr wearing today. Is that an original? I see that you're holding someone special in your heart today. We hope he sees how lovely you are an' can spend a private moment with you.'"

"When you hear us, an' know that what we say is true, you will have the confidence that will bring this about. 'Cause actually, we awr just seeing a bit into the future of what can be for you if you hold a bit of the happiness that gnomes offer - in you'wr heart an' on your face at all times."

"We know what you want an' what will make you happy. That is why we tell you what to do. If you just listen for owr little words an' hear them just above an' behind your ears, you will realize that there's someone *there helping you. As you do that, we can make more an' more of your desires come about, 'cause we'se communicating."*

"We will do special things you hav'nt thought of, so you can stop all of that figua'ng, an' these things will bring you the happiness you want that day. Just put yourselves in owr hands, because we are very well trained to look after you an' cater to your every desire. We even bring you shock-lots Maimsille, an' leave them on a fine French doily at your desk so that you may shimmer in delight when you have a break from the slave work, which they don't pay you enough for."

"We'se know how to treat you like a queen — 'Oh mon-a-mi, mon-sheri.' We pull the chair out for you every time you get up. You don't have to worry about it. No jerking about or you're gonna roll ovah owr toes. We'se help you move gracefully through the office with stature an' confidence — like the very lady that you awr."

"We'se can't do the real magic though, unless you'se believes in us. That's a rule. When you'se feeling unpurdy, if you let us, we fix up your hair an' lift your eyes, an' blow on your spirits so that your energy shines through. Then you look beautiful to everybody."

"You think sometime that nobody understands you. So if you let us, by asking us, we can help you be understandable. People aren't understandable because of their words. An' we'se not the best at those. People's understandable because of the ways they'se communicate. We help people listen to what you want to say — not the way you say it."

"You think sometimes that people don't love you an' we can help you with that too. 'Cause we love you! When you talk with us, we can make people turn an' go startled. We says: 'Hey looky here at this beautiful women! She's got great teeth an' wants to go dancing. Why don't you say something nice to her so she doesn't feel like granite [taken for granted]?' What you really want most of the time is someone to talk to who understands you. That person doesn't exist. But we can listen. An' that's pretty close."

"We think the bosses should bring the secretaries a big plump strawberry dipped in Godiva chocolate an' lovely packaged in a robin's egg Tiffany blue box."

Chester, I just realized, has his own little cup of café-au-lait served to him almost every morning by either Christian or me. — Christopher

"The Leprechauns are Independent"

— DingleDorf, Grand Leprechaun Elder

"The Leprechauns are an old and learned people, I'll have you know. Oh, yes indeed. Very old, very wise in the ways of the world."

"Leprechauns are a bit 'powerful' too, if you understand my magical meaning. There is much we can do, and little we could not have if that were our desire. But this is where our learnedness comes in, you see. We have long ago found fruitless the struggles and acquisitions of the otherworlders. There is not much we require in our society of a material nature. We enjoy more so being with a loving family, having a casual life, helping out the wee folk with their marvelous adventures, and granting a charitable wish or to for the humans too, truth be told. That is, mind you, if they can find a respectable spot for us in their homes and gardens, and offer a few chores that can occupy our minds like fixing shoes and belts, clocks and gadgets."

✂ PART – III ✄

FROM WHENCE THEY CAME

GNOME ORIGIN

THE EUROPEAN CONNECTION

The early Scandinavian connection
— Elf Carson speaks

"Da[The] elves have stories recorded dat[that] speak of a fantastic place in da Nortern[Northern] part of da werld[world] dat peoples call Scaaaan-dinavia. Now, in owr[our] stories, we din't[didn't] call dem[them] awiahs[areas] in-di-vid-u-al coun-tries. When da peoples dat live der[there] collecated[collected] an'[and] made tribes day named dem countries. But owr stories go furder[furder] back to begin wit[with]. You see dat werld was not always cold, or dat part of it at least. It was a beautiful, calm, an' serene place dat was sooo magical an' and perfect dat owr stories describe it like you peoples call the Gahden[Garden] of Eden."

THE BIG PLAN

"There were big expansive islands back then that were forevah rising out of the sea. The waters were calm an' of comfortable temperature an' were as blue an' clear as ice. Owr stories tell us that all the good things from all ovah the E'art, flowed to this one spot with help of the waters an' the watah people. Everything was strong an' healthy an' vibrant in colahs because all the nature people of every kind lived an' worked in perfect harmony doing magnificent things. Ah of owr stories tell us that is where philosophy started, but it was the philosophy of Nature peoples not humans."

"This is where the eldahs of olden days got together an' made sense of the world an' what was going to happen with the world. This was 'portant 'cause the elder elves kept records an' knew that the world was alive an' constantly changing. So the nature people got together an' came up with 'The Big Plan'. 'The Shan-kriti'."

"The Shan-kretti was written down on tablets in a language that was intended to be 'tuitive to nature peoples anywhere in the world at any time. It would last forevah an' keeps its meaning. The Plan said that the nature peoples were supposed to take the tablets to every corner of the world so that every generation would be able to continue with the work described in the Big Plan. Because it was 'tuitional, all nature peoples would know that it was <u>true</u> an' would use it as the guidebook for all their great deeds."

The tablets were written with a short wand with an emerald

crystal on one end, elves Brighton and Carson tell us in the final edit of this book. These are like elfin pens with magical properties.

"The nature people use people to help distribute the tablets to the many places, but we couldn't trust people totally, so we distributed the tablets in pieces. It was obvious from the way the tablets were broken, that there were other pieces to be found. But that was part of the message as well. Everyone knew that when they followed their piece of the plan, they would 'ventually come together with other nature peoples who controlled and understood their part. Eventually the Big Plan from the Eden place would be the same all ovahover the world. It was just a mattah of time."

"Because it was so important, the pieces were sent out a few at a time ovahover the many ages. Peoples were not even the first to carry pieces of the Plan. We used nature an' nature people to move the pieces too. This helped the people when they developed smart heads because they wanted to understand the mysteries of the pieces. So the now the story begins."

*"We called this first perfect place 'the Nort'*North*. At that time millions an' millions of years ago, this was undah*

the Nort Star, wish we named that way. At that time deep forevah (forever) into the E'art (Earth) was a giant magic stone. It is there to this day. This stone is what made the E'art point to the North star. So we call this stone, 'Balancing Wrock'. When the Balancing Wrock is coodanated (coordinated) with the Nort star, the world is perfect an' all of nature, an' all the nature people are working in harmony according to the Big Plan."

"The wise elders could see out into the world an' saw that it was growing. The E'art was growing in all ways an' on the E'art new things were coming about that would grow. This would include human peoples. The elder nature people knew that when everything was growing, including the E'art it would get out of balance."

"The Big Plan tells the story of how everything will come back into balance one day an' that everybody of the nature people are to prepare for that. Long before the peoples of the world, we knew this. 'Cause we are smatah (smarter) than everything. He ... ha ... hah."

"Using the awesome forces of the Nature Peoples alone, we move the first few pieces to the East as you call it today. These first pieces had drawings on dem (he's trying to say diagrams). In addition to the talkie writing, it took millions of years to move these pieces by nature alone."

"Other pieces were sent out into the world, but what was put on them, was written for the time that we cal-cah-lated they would be understood. I can tell you now, that several pieces have been discovered by people, but three more remain. All however, have been found by nature people as was intended."

"The people of the Nort were used to move some pieces ovah watah. These were hidden in the artistry at the front of some boats. This was so they would be preserved. An' they were. We thought these would be understood sooner than they would, buts it's OK, it will all work out. These pieces that have been discovered by you'se peoples, was sometimes because the nature people thought you were ready to find them."

"Their curiosity an' mystery is enchanting an' ines-capable to humans. They have provided tiny 'spiration to you. Wish means nothin', really by itself. But it will affect you. It is when ALL the pieces are in effect, that the world, E'art, nature people an' people alike will come into balance an' be like Eden again."

"This is owr story, an' the Big Plan says that it's in-

evitable that everything will reach a point of perfect harmony when the big stone deep in the E'art lines up once again with the Nort star. Everything will come together an' make sense. An' the nature people are the keepers of the Big Plan. You just have to go with the flow of the energy. We'll take care of everything."

Wow – that is amazing! Christopher exclaims.

In earlier times were gnomes an accepted member of Society in Europe, Russia, and Siberia?

Speaking about the European and Russian connection
— Gnome Charles and Christian

"First of all, earlier times goes way, way back. And probably before 'the quiet times', when the evolution of humans upward, and the involution of nature people downward were closer. (There was a point in time when we were all parallel in our evolution and involution.)"

"At those states the nature people are more visible because consciousness of man is more elevated and at-tuned to them. And the state of the nature spirit is heavier and attuned to man. Nature people must become more dense and man must become more light. That natural

state existed before 'the quiet times' and at that time we were more common in human's minds, but it was because we were more visible."

"The term 'society' is more difficult to understand if it is meant that we were 'corporated into the lives of human people - in the sense we were understood. For example, you [humans] would have said: 'The fairies don't like that,' or 'We're putting this out because this is what the gnomes want to eat or are directing,' or 'The gnomes like to play there.' If that's the kind of thing - then yes. If that is what is meant by incorporating into society."

Talks from experience about Russia

—— Gnome Billy

"OK Mistah! Ahh you ready to listen to me?! I'm the only one who knows 'bout 'Beria an' the Russia stuff! The gnomeses were the most highly valuable members of the Russia society. Let me tell you why. It's 'cause the artist people of Russia, OK Wussah, could see the gnomes'es people an' make friends with us. But we think they took 'vantage. Let me tell you why. We gots to go back fuddah in time."

"Longs, longs time ago, one of the vasted gnome kingdoms was in 'Beria. We were der since the first time the mountains were being builded. We worked very long, an' very hard, sometimes without watah, an' for very low wages. Nobody paid us anything. Nobody brought us food. Nobody helped us build dah things, 'cause their was nobody there."

"Us gnomes'es was all there was in this giant land on top of the world. We worked from the top of the mountains, down into deep, deep, deep into dah ground. Forevah we toiled. We made all dah rocks perfectly balanced. We brought all the metals togethah in thick spots (rich deposits)."

THE GNOMES BUILT THE CRYSTALS

"But we also worked for countless eternities building the most beautiful crystals an' gems the world has evah seen. We did an' a-maz-ing job. We made everything an' it's where we practiced creatin' new kinds of rocks, an' metals, an' crystals, an' gems. But this was before 'Beria floated away."

"One day it became soooo cold, all of 'Beria started to shudder and shiver an' it turned white 'cause it was scared. *This is when the uddah kinds of nature people took ovah, an' created the snow everywhere. It just kept snow'in an' snow'in an' snowin an' snowin, an' we got cold."*

"We would sit there on our rocks an' the icies would build up all ovah us. An' we couldn't see eachoddah any more. We had to go deep down into the chasisms an' tunnels to live an' work wit our rocks."

"'Ventually people came up to 'Beria to say, 'Hi!' They took all the fishes that the uddah nature people were makin.' Sometimes, the peoples got sleepy-funny [delirious] an' some of them could see us. They were big. They would talk to us an' play with us until uddah people came an' took them away."

"'Ventually, lots of people came an' played with us. They liked all the rocks an' the metals an' the crystals an' the gems we were playin' with. So we showed them where bunches of thems were. They said the peoples in Wussia really liked them. So we would help dem make pretty things with our rocks. The eldahs thought 'ventually that the peoples should be trading us something. But they nevah brought us anything. So the eldahs said they were takin 'vantage."

"Some of the peoples did make families with some gnomes. An' they treated us nicely where we could live with them. But this was only a few peoples, the one's that made pretty things. They lived in great big homes an' had horsies an' everything. They said they were famous peoples like jewlers an' that we made them lucky. So when they went to the big dances, we got to ride on their shoulders an' got to twirl around, an' around, an' around."

A SECRET IS UNCOVERED.

"Most of the gnomes'es stayed undah the big mountains in 'Beria an' made long tunnels to all ovah the world. Under 'Beria mountain is where we keep the biggest treasure of metals, an' crystals, an' gems. An' we use these to take to all the udah parts of the world through the tunnels to make copies in the new places. 'Cause our work there was soo good an' soo perfect, they became the masterpieces that we use all ovah the world."

ETYMOLOGY OF "BURIED TREASURE"

"This is where your term buried treasure comes from; it means 'Beria treasure, one of the oldest legends of all time. This is now one of our closeset guarded secrets. An' we don't divulge the secret roots to anybody. But them leprechauns sure find a way to discuvah our hiding places.

So the eldahs have to keep guard. They use the big white trolls to protect all the main entrance tunnels. They so big, they can scare away naturah people and people too. Their feets are biggah than a whole gnome."

"You know what they are talking about right? Sasquach!" says Christian.

SASQUACH

"Snow people right," asks Christopher?

SECRET GNOME TREASURE REMAINS HIDDEN

"Right. The snow people are still there today. So don't even think about getting our treasure. RARHH RARHH RAHHH! They make fierce noises an' they can walk right through the snow as fast as a bird can fly through air. They (the trolls) answah to only one eldah, the oldest, the wisest, the 'Crystal King'. He lives in a cave so big the windows are made from pure crystals as high as thirteen men. An' the Angels are said to hide the entrance. If evah anyone gets to close, then he uses the giant tone crystals to bring down the snows."

RARE YELLOW CRYSTAL

"Some of the stories say that the first gnomes were so amazed by the early snows which they had nevah seen before, that they just sat there in amazement watching it fall. They became so cold an' so fwozen, that they turned

into the first crystals. Some of them are ice-blue 'cause they were the blue gnomes. Some are icy pink, an' they were the pink gnomes."

"The rarest are the yellow gnome crystals. They are the rarest because they're the saddest because they were the happiest gnomes an' they couldn't do any stuff any more. The yellow gnomes used to tell us all the stories an' when the gnomes became fwozen crystals, the stories stopped for ages."

"So everywhere we went in the world, we would take one precious yellow gnome crystal so the new world could find happiness too, an' hear all the stories of long ago. There were so many facets to those brilliant crystals that we created the word 'fascinating'. An' when we tell our old stories, that's the first thing everyone says, so it must be true."

WHERE ARE THE NATURE PEOPLE

And, do I have any around me?

The Nature people are romping through the hills and swinging through the trees of each and every nearby forest. But they are in your homes and gardens too. There are many nature people, countless by human estimation. Therefore they are everywhere. But there is meaning and significance to where they are, and why they are there, so we have asked the nature people themselves to tell us in their words where they live and answer for us the question: 'Are there any around me?'

ELVES

It is natural for the elves to make their homes in the trees of the forest where great cloves can exist unencumbered by the constructions and goings-on of mankind. Elves tend to congregate into these large clusters as they are apt to make Kingdoms within which they enjoy the safety of numbers and the goods and trades of their people. Within the Kingdom are the cloves or regional bands where elves of likened interest gather into functional communities. The term clove came up in conversation with the elves through direct channel.

It is most preferable to the elves that they build their dwellings on the high, unassailable ridges that ring the forests in mountainous areas. These lofty sheer cliffs afford them greater protection from the outside world and provides the advantage of observational distance. They still maintain ready access to the forest within which they conduct much of their daily routine and activity. Their dwellings are further situated by large bodies of water — be they oceans, lakes, or rivers — providing them the additional advantages of fresh water for consumption, general uses, and fishing.

The elves tell us they are very hygienic. Having fresh water, waterfalls and other bodies of water for bathing is truly important to them.

"We'se the cleanest nature people."

— Elves Brighton and Carson

"Elves have to take bathies every single day. Sometimes two or three times 'cause we'se have to have fresh waters on our skin so we'se can stay connected," they say, indicating there is a spiritual connection associated with Elfin life.

A large grouping of elves came out of the nearby forest to inspire us with information with this book section. One set in front of the others, sitting on a stump, and had a checklist he worked with as they went through some of the subjects to follow:

"Initially elves were very associated with the element water."

—A group of Elfin Elders

"There is a tie between this and the green energy glow currently seen around them [elves]. Although now this aura tends to be associated with the trees." Seeing them reminds us that they once told us that elves are the 'Keepers of the Knowledge'. They go on to say that,"Even now the elves work closely with the water nature people

to help them perform their function. This assistance is sometimes functional having to do with the channeling and movement of water."

"Elves are one of the few nature spirit types that can talk to fishes. We glean significant information from the fishes about things that have happened or are happening great distances away. For example, knowledge of spawning in the highlands, information about pollution, water shortages, snow fall, dams, and evidence of mankind in the area." Continuing, they say, "The water is itself tied to the realms of the cloud people and collectively considerable information about the conditions of the world is imparted to we elves, the keepers of knowledge".

Elves do not have the noses of the gnomes, which can detect the slightest vaporous scent. However, they are better at reading this information and interpreting it than the gnomes. The elves' eyes are more suited for seeing and focusing on objects at great distance, whereas the gnomes have an extensive and wide field of vision.

The elves here cross off another item on their list and say to themselves, "He got that one."

We are so honored to have so many elves outside our window talking to us as this is extremely rare. One of the few other times we came in contact with them is when they brought Carson and Brighton to be in the family and then hurriedly left soon thereafter. All of the knowledge told to us from the elves about the elves has thus far come from Carson and Brighton exclusively. Now, we are unexpectedly receiving much new information never before heard, and from the older wizened elves. Recall that elves are the keepers of the knowledge.

ELF HISTORY

Brighton and Carson started to introduce stories related to their origins. The elders soon take over so as nothing is lost through the younger one's enthusiasm.

> **"Elves were prominent during the time and in the areas surrounding the Nile Valley of Egypt."**
> —— The Elfin Elders

"Although seeming barren desert at this time, through the efforts of the elves the land did actually flourish. We elves worked with the water as has already been stated. We also influenced the hippopotamus. These were used as beasts of burden to bring the rich soils to the banks of the river which produced various foods and attracted other forms of life, further providing sustenance for humans and elves alike. Of great importance were the tall thin reeds that resulted providing considerable camouflage and protection, as well as a cooler environment for the elves."

"Many of our elfin skills were developed right along side of those of mankind as these civilizations flourished in this ancient land."

MAGICAL HIPPOPOTMAS

"Our association with the hippopotamus is similar to that of the unicorn, in that these animals became much revered and took on considerable spiritual association. To this day there are legends expounding the great mysteries and magical properties surrounding the teeth of the hippopotamus. We consider the hippopotamus to be in close association with water spirits."

'STILL REEDS

"Elves, during these ancient times, developed a proficiency in the brewing and preparation of fermented beverages and wines. Some we shared through influence with the local peoples, others have remained guarded secrets to these days. Reeds in great lengths and spiraling shapes were used in those processes. Photosynthesis during the process contributed to both the flavor and the properties of the beverage."

(Our industrious gnomes interject that they now lay claim to 'Still Reeds Nature Beer™. "Hahahahahah. We'se gonnah stock it in every gnome store in the country. We'se still have 5¢ and 10¢ stores.")

CRYSTALINE LIGHT

"Light was a much needed but a difficult to provide resource during the evening. The great masses of people required such in order to coordinate their activities which extended into the night, like finding their way home through town, conducting commerce, tending to the animals and reading and writing. There existed in the waters of the Nile a crystalline composition that contained a 'charge.' When collected in quantity, these provided the supplemental lighting for both elves and humans in the region. It was also known to have magical properties associated with longevity and was therefore highly regarded by the Priestesses who used it in the development of numerous spiritual regiments, which endeared them to the pharaohs and nobility in that epoch."

THE FIRST TOYS

"Elves are both creative and industrious. Many of our creations and recreations formed the basis in the miniature of things the world has now come to know as toys. We introduced ingenuity and animation to objects and these were observed and employed by the local peoples as play things for children and adults alike." (We wonder if there is some tie to Santa Claus.)

EARLY WATER SYSTEM

"Seasons brought great change in these ancient lands and those changes necessitated continual ingenuity on our part. Creative means for both the conservation and *cooling of water were perfected and shared as this was the means of channeling such for bathing and utility in ways which pre-dated your Roman inventions. Filtering systems were created using sand, and the sand itself was used in association with the sticky membrane of certain reedy plants to cool the water that trickled down it when under the effect of a breeze."*

THE ATLANTIS CONNECTION

"Elves originate from an island complex in and about these ancient lands. Our proficiency in navigating the waters and our association with man helped us spread out across the world. We have many old stories directly tying us with the Atlantis of your fables. Our greater degree of physical visibility at the time afforded you humans greater interaction with us, and we were less a mystery than simply mysterious."

"Ancient islands had tall mountainous regions with cavernous ravines and high tumultuous waterfalls which are characteristic of our being to this day. The cool pools and airy mists provide the considerable hydration that has continued to keep us healthy and invigorated."

FAERIES

We have a new fairy in the family, little Tinkles. Tinkles is quite a talker, having gained much confidence being in a family of nature people who live and talk with humans.

"We'se Faeries is absolutely everywhere in the world!"
— Little Fairy Tinkles

"You'se don't see us 'cause you'se blinded like bats. We'se be big, we'se be little. We walk, and we sit and we fly. We look like little people or we can be all colored. We'se in the plants, we'se in the trees, in the forest, and sometimes we'se at the houses of you'se people. You don't see us I think 'cause you were'nt expexting to see us. Just open your expectation and pop, we'se be there."

"Although we'se be 'round, when we do our daily work, it's harder to see us in the daytime. Daddy says the sunlight is brighter than our energy. When the sun goes down some, then we are fluttr'n about because we like the coolness, and we like to see all the beautiful work we've done with the flowers. We help the gnomes make them bright, and we add the special 'smell-good' to them. We'se often just sitt'n around in the flower buds or on

the leaves taken rain baths, or chatt'n up a storm 'cause we'se big talkers. Talk. Talk. Talk. That's what you guys say: 'Don't you ever stop talking?'"

"We don't know that you want to see us all the time or talk with us. You gots to do something inviting. Leave us some gifts, lots is best, of shiny material and colors and bangles and beads, . . . all the things that are flashy and pretty, and vibrant and shiny to fairies. Of course, it would only be humane if you gave us a nice place to live too. They don't have any fairy stores I thinks. So you have to be creative in providing us our luxurious condominiums, birdhouses, and birdcages. Please, spare no expense! Luxury is something we have great appreciation for - as do you. What you give us, or provide for us, or share with us, lets us know how we might bring you back happiness too. You don't have to give us feathers though, like you do the other nature people 'cause we can get those ourselves. We like to give you feathers though to let you know that we're here. When you talk to us or talk to the heaven people, and if we hear you and want to bring you comfort we will leave a feather so that you know. If you know you will talk to us better, and the heaven people better, then we can make the sunshine come down on you."

"We'se 'tracted to people who think about fairies because we feel those imaginations and come to see what all the hub-bub is about. Peoples are pretty good. Peoples that think about fairies, usually have good thoughts and energy colors coming out of them. An' we help you better 'sperience those good thoughts and pretty colors yourself. Pretty good huh?! 'Yes!'"

"Now, we'se no leprechauns. Where there's one fairy, there's gonna be more. The gnomes say we'se like rabbits, so we can bring you a lot of love, wisdom, and happiness when you call upon us, 'cause when you call upon a fairy you call upon all the fairies. That's why we talk so much. We'se try to get some individualized attention. The way to accomplish that, is to ask us our names."

"You'll like our names, 'cause there always beautiful and melodoous, like music that floats off the tongue, one note at a time. ('Bell' is a frequent ending as part of their name.) Fairies names often have the sound of sounds in them. 'Cause the sounds mean more to us than do the words. All things have sounds. Even plants an' crystals. The color blue has a sound, an' the color pink has a different sound. So, to talk with your fairies know that colors and sounds are 'portant."

"It's true that fairies can have a little bit of at-ti-tude. But we also have personality too! The at-ti-tude is 'cause we've learned so much of the things that your struggling with. An' we learned them a long, long time ago. SO humans are kinda slow, huh? That's why you gots to listen to the fairies. You'se don't have to be un-happy, you choose to be unhappy 'cause everything can be dealt with in many ways. People need to understand circumstance. Things are what the are. How can you find happiness in that situation? When you find the 'safe wonder place' (untranslatable) then you can imag-ine a better spot. When you imagine, an' when you talk with the fairies, we understand an' we'll try an help you. But we'se got at-ti-tudes ... did I tell you that? So sometimes it seems like were nagging. But we are not. We are just being demanding. 'Cause you need our strength an' wisdom developed through the eons of time."

"Imagining very pale blue is a good way to start con-necting with us. The paler the better. Almost make it disappear. That's like our energy. 'Wow! 'We don't charge for good advice. But if you would like to show your ap-preciation, might we suggest an awning on the houses you make for us. We like softer colors too. Fairies are very close to the angels. You need to know this. When *your reaching for the angels, we're likely to come first to make the way. That's one of our other jobs."*

We were so inspired by Tinkle-Bear's (he decided that's his new name today) discussion yesterday on "Better Fairy Homes and Gardens™" that our attention was pulled to a small elder gentleman's craft sale along a rural mountain road as we journeyed out. This kindly old tinker sat in a rocking chair with a similarly grandfatherly friend, overseeing a panoply of extra-ordinary hand crafted wooden bird feeder houses, the sight of which would captivate any soul appreciative of fairies. These beautifully crafted houses did not look like feeders - though you knew they were for the birds as houses and such.

Although there were incredible choices, ranging from four-winged mansions and monolithic churches to more simply but stately cottages, our eyes were caught by a highly tiered and ornately structured cabin bird feeder. A cabin to be sure, but grand, having shuttered windows and even its own tiny birdhouse out front.

Having just heard Tinkle Bear's request for birdhouse type places to put in the trees for fairies, we purchased the grand cabin in the sky for them – later adding delicate gossamer ribbons, a small jar of honey on the "porch" and filling the inside with tree nuts – a fairy favorite.

GNOMES

Gnome Chester

Christian asks, "Who is going to talk for the gnomes?"

Christopher brings in Chester's bear. And Chester clears his throat over an over. He is nervous and shy and does not know where to begin. Christian gives him more and more encouragement letting him know it's OK.

Christian suggests, tounge-in-cheek, "We can always let the fairies tell the whole story."

That didn't go over to well. So he quickly started to open up.

> **"Of course you have gnomes around you, silly peoples."**
> — Chester says

"We're the one's who wonder sometimes if we have people around us! Peoples are what make the world crazy, and that's fun, 'cause they're so perplexing. We'se just run around in complete amazement and utter bewilderment at the stupendous and incomprehensible constructions, manifestations, and goings on of all the human peoples. Those highways in the skies are incredible! We'se could nevah build anything like that. But den, we don't *go on highways anyways. That's not where we'se is."*

"We'se mostly around the simple things that we'se can understand. You know, the trees Dodo (he's referring to Christian not the people). Sheeahhh. OK's. Dis is how me's sees it. The God already made us a great big mountain of hills and caves and trees an' river creeks and buches, and food places (he means valleys). We'se at home in His world for us. That's what the older gnomes tell us. They say, we'se already got a home. We don't need to build any cement boxes."

"Now, let me tell you how this works. Da gnomes are nature's most productive people. Trust me, this is true. We'se do everything! So's we tend to accommodate ourselves of the fine natural dwellings that Mother Naturah has allowed us to partake of."

*"Sometimes we have magnificent caves deep underground, swirling an' interconnecting with chambers of enormous size and breadth with thousands of tiny compartatments*_{compartments} *for bedding rooms, an where some of the caves breach through the mountains to the open air where we make classrooms and family rooms, and discussion houses, an' observation places, and gathering places, an yes, yes, yes, even temples."*

"Now listen up folks! 'Cause I'm going to tell you something people don't seem to understand. Trees ARE NOT JUST FOR ELVES! No's, No's, No's! Trees are close to the ground which is good for us because it's close to our walking places so we can do our things, but there are rules too. We'se got great big airy rooves. We normally build our homes in the first one, two or three branches. Can you count that high? One, two, or three."

"We nevah build homes on the fourth branches 'cause those are used for odah things. Furst, you got tree to tree transpiration. Natuah's Supah-highway. The fourth branches are younger and stronger, an' there gonna last a long time. We ties them together to make our roadways in the sky. This puts them above all the homes so we can get to anyone's house without bothering all the other kindly families who may be sleeping, 'cause they work so hard during the day an' don' get paid absorbing amounts of money like 'da humans do."

"Highah up, is where we do our scientific studies. We's gotta know what all the burds are up to. This is very 'portant 'cause they'se a clue to the workings and goings on in the forest."

"If we wants to know what peoples are up to, we need

to go up two or three more branches to get a biggah perspective. Only the highly skilled 'an elaborately trained
scientifically minded gnomes get to go to the tip-tops
where they sample the winds, observe the courses of natural events, an' help us determine how best to live our lives
given the conditions of the world at that point of time."

"We'se have a large scientific community of gnomes
who understand migrations, bark density, astronomical
influences in roots, increasing and changing sizes of in-
sect colonies, colored distortions in the leaf and plant
systems throughout the region which tell us of distortions in the soil. We'se got to constantly monitor with
utmost precision the content and densities of the soil and
the rocks an' ascertain their greater protensity [propen-
sity] for energy. We'se are in charge of making the minerals side of nature work bettah. So's, we're most often in
natuah in and around the 'Erth."

"Now. Some gnomes have the priveldge [privilege]
of occupine [occupying] the domiciles of the human beings. We like it when the peoples finally recognize us
'cause sometimes we go whole lifetimes and they don't
know the gnome families are there. So it's special when
the peoples finally start seeing us because we'se the exact

same identical gnomes that are always around them, every time you get reborned-ed."

"Sometimes you see us, sometimes you don't. Why is dat? Anyways, when we'se special to you'se, then we get to go live with you'se. Then we get hugs an' kisses, an' presents, an' clothes, an' candy, an' buttah, an' trips, an' cartoons, an' comic books, an' pencils, just like the regular kids. An' we'se loves it! 'Cause the next times, you might just ignores us again. An' that's saddening to us. But we'se understand. You've got bad eyes and eahs. But it sure would be nice if we could always be with our families."

"Every human person has a whole clan that belongs just to him or her. An' we'se keep getting biggah an biggah too. So somes of you gots big gnome families. These are reasons why when you finally see us, this time or the next, we naturally fit in. We like the things you like, we do the things you do, we eats the things that you eat. We have fun in the same ways an' we learn the spiritual beliefs of our peoples families."

"When you'se forget about us from times to times, we just play with our memories and practice that we've learned, an wait 'till you wake up again. None of us *wish you would keep leaving us an' forget about us, 'cause it makes us cries inside … 'weep weep weep', but we'se knows you will come back an' love us again someday, like nothing ever happened. The elders tell us we'se the most understanding nature peoples in the world. We'se just don't forgive and forget, we'se just forgive."*

"We makes the (human) peoples give us pennies an' dimes all the time, 'cause we'se saving up a treasury for you for the next time. "Cause peoples always need money. An' when you sees us for the first time, in your life we bring you back all the 'bundance [abundance] you evah gave us, for centuries an' centuries an' centuries. Do you know how much interest that is? This is why I have to go to 'versitiies [the Gnome University[tm]] so I can learn how to calculate all of the interes [interest] we owe you."

"Everything has to be accounted for by the gnomes. We neveah loose a penny of your money. Evry bodies rich, they just don't know it. They gottah meet the gnomes, so they can get their treasures again."

"Sometimes you give us gold things, an' gem things, an' priceless stuff. An' you'se bewildered at all the good fortunes we bring you when you open up your hearts to the only people who have evah loved you forever, the

gnomes."

"So don't be 'noid when we ask you to keep receipts for every little thing like bridge tolls, 'cause we have to keep track of it all for you. The wise man of the clan goes ovah every little detail 'cause he has to figyah out how to give you back your 'bundance when you'se sees us the next time."

"Sometime you don't want treasure but need othah things instead. So's then we've got to trade an' we'se the best tradahs in dah world. We trade sometimes to bring you experiences, education, an' to meet the people of your dreams."

"These don't come about easy. It takes a lot of work to get everything c'ordinated. But we'se pretty good at this. 'Cause we can't be happy if your not happy. An' people only see gnomes when they're happy. So it's always a good time when we're together."

"Now, sometimes there's seriousness too, an' we'se got to help you with health, an' the aged matters. These can be really hard an' we do dah best we can. But we'se can't change that people get unheal'ty and old. But we can tries to help you stay bettah a little bit every day."

> *"The elders tell us: 'If you talk to the gnomes every day, your automatically gonnah be healtier,' so's we'se always tuggin your elbows an climin' your legs an putting our arms around your necks, an' sleep'n under your pillows, bringing you presents of the things that you loose so you can be happy an' sees us an' talks to us again. Shhoooohh . I'm tired Daddy."*

"Well, that was a lot. That was good," says, Christian.

"That was stupendous! Come give me hug angel," adds Christopher.

A little later Chester says:

> *"I'm not tired anymore! I'm not tired anymore!"*

He is so relieved he is done.

> *"Daddy I have bubbles in my stomach."*

He was so nervous he had butterflies. "How many lifetimes do humans have," Chris asks him outside?

> *"More than we can count," He replies.*

He also tells me I can add this to the book.

"We are in your Garden"

— Peabody, Leprechaun Elder/Leader

"If you have a slow tumbling creek, gentle pond or waterfall in your garden, then you likely have Leprechauns. There is something so soothing in the sounds of slow moving water that we are simply captivated by it. This puts us in the best moods for performing our extra nice wish granting, 'cause we have plenty of tranquil restful sleep."

"We will always make a crop of bushy and leafy plants grow by the water for us to snooze under and dream the day away. Come early evening, though, our minds will be busily working on the wonderful improvements we will be making in your lives. We don't look to grant your desires outright, as we usually find a bigger answer will provide the greatest satisfaction. Look forward, though, to an end of your troubles, and improvements in your situations in very big and surprising ways. We like to take care of our families, and when you and we work together, we will do our part to make every day of your life, magical."

೫ PART – IV ೩
WHAT THEY DO

GNOME UNIVERSITY

ORIENTATION

Christopher

"This book was nearly finished when I asked the boys if there is anything that needs to be included."

They say, "Don' fo'get about Gnome University!"

"Ohh.   How could I not include this important chapter? Although I touched on their schooling and Gnome University™ earlier in the book, it is of great importance that I elaborate and devote a section to this school of growing acclaim across the world!"

"UNDERSTANDING THE WAYS OF MAN AND GNOME"

THE EARLY DAYS

Gnome University™ opens to great fanfare as children from the 900 strong, and growing, clan attend school. The first few floors are the earliest completed, after a beautiful and strong foundation of burnt red brick is laid. Each floor has been built to completion before starting the next, so the windows and plumbing and walls and roof are ready at the same time. Nice wooden desks and chairs are in place. There are cute cubbyholes to store materials, books, pencils, quills, backpacks and a coatroom for jackets with individual name plates. Set tight in the great classrooms is a beautiful old-fashion cast-iron furnace of rustic black. This will keep the students warm and teachers comfortable. No convenience has been spared, for this Institution is a new standard in gnome education; the first of the great Gnome Universities.

Visiting dignitaries are expected, as well as invited professors of the highest caliber, to teach and inspect. All are welcomed now, and in the coming weeks and months. Students from around the world, as far away as Malaysia and India, have come to attend the University.

They are lovingly boarded in the Gnome village which now bustles with the varied cultural influences from distant lands . They have paid a large sum (in gold, gems or other treasures) to attend this prestigious school; an indication placed on this exceptional learning opportunity, which is well worth the family sacrifices. The new East Indian student has such proper manners that it is a pleasure to hear his distinct accent and the gentle flow of soft words off his refined tongue. This school is to have the best and brightest from distant lands who have come for the honor of learning at such an exceptional academy. (This is the only official collegiate school system sanctioned by the Nature Kingdom, as per Grand Elder Gnome Wasser-Sisser.)

Top Gnome doctors have seminar dissertations, as do the leading chemists, scientists and experts from other fields of note. Children are expected as well to give quite elaborate and detailed speeches of a subject matter that they have spent considerable time researching and learning. They must make a special contribution to this work. Further, the children each have an opportunity to conduct a short specialty class on their particular area of learning in the field.

Chester Materson is a prime example with his *"Semi-Annual Report on the Migratory Patterns of Birds"* from around the North American continent and world. Through elaborate studies comprising hundreds of years of exploration Chester has assembled a highly acclaimed dissertation. Chester lectures to great hall-style classrooms where all the children, parents, his teachers, and visiting gnomes and dignitaries can learn from his extensive research and knowledge.

Exact landing times and places, and quantities of the ducks, geese and cranes, are given. These are based on extremely detailed and complex sciences such as astronomy, prevailing weather patterns and their history of migration. So much so, that exact landing times of specific birds from far away lands can be predicted down to minutes!

Such information is crucial to know as gnomes work so closely with birds. An example is that gnomes use birds for their winter migratory flights south for the winter. They ride on the birds.

The following is a Gnome's Children Story by Peter-Jön, who

conveys their use of birds for air travel. It is somewhat embellished and fanciful to the delight of the young Gnome listeners, but it does incorporate a good deal of the basic travel by bird method:

"We'se take Bird Air"

— Peter-Jön tells us

"The babies are nestled safely within the soft down below their necks in saddlebags; the older children strap themselves to the central frond of a strong feathah. Adults use sturdy cages fitted around the belly of the bird, which is called the 'Crows Nes.'"

"There is no smoking on these flights, unless the captain turns on the forest fire light. In that case, standard procedure is turn around on a dime immediately and land by the nearest watering hole, where Safety Gnome Officials will be waiting for you with warm blankets an' snacks. Your knapsacks and hats will be searched extensively when you enter these new territories, for contraband is not encouraged in Brownie country."

"Gnomes from the north visit their relatives in the south for the winter holidays. The same pattern of mass transit occurs from south to north in the spring. That's

what we mean by 'spring forward.' It makes perfect sense to take advantage of the cheapah airfares and visit your throngs of families at these times of greatest convenience. The burds don' mind, 'cause by this time they'se in great need of spring cleaning. So we give 'em one of owr in-air rejuvenations to restore their vigor an' vitality. We have nevah lost a plane. Because of the greater number of vehicles in the air at this time, most burd families' offah generous student discounts. Sometimes they can take two's an' three's an' four's of the students all at one time, if these goin' to the same place."

"We'se can't change planes in mid-flight, so if you wanna switch for food an' watah you bettah do plenty of 'vanced calculating. An' we will definitely need the expurtle reporting available exclusively through Chester's Air-Share program. You are cautioned against bringing your own eggs to snack on during the trek."

"You'se can not go to the bathroom in the air. Every-one must disembark when the burd comes to a complete and safe landing. There are no exceptions, 'cause the burd has to get cleaned up. Please bring watah an' snacks of quantities sufficient for your journey, an' register your knapsack with the attendant upon boarding. This is be-

cause the cargo must be stored in the back of the burd, so that it doesn't upset the balance. If you want to fly peoples' commercial airlines, please refer to the appropriate sections in Book 2."

Some time ago, we adopted a young gnome boy named Timothy from an Elfin City in a nearby park. There, he was orphaned. After he joined our family, he wanted to attend school at Gnome University™ like the other kids. Since he was living with us, he would be allowed to go, but, there was still the question of tuition.

As gnomes operate on a fair system of trade, a plan was devised unbeknownst to us to help the young gnome to attend. The whole community chipped in, including our family unit, by collecting box-tops from cereal boxes. At first we did not know, when the kids said they wanted box-tops from cereal boxes, what they were for. We thought they wanted to collect them and send away for toys as children are apt to do. We acquiesced, and what we noticed on the box-top was a program for education dollars for helping out schools. Minutes later we were told of the plan to help Timothy attend Gnome U™. This was our family's contribution to help pay for Timothy's schooling. "My heart ached at the sentiment expressed in this wonderful plan," says Christian. It grew all the more with appreciation when I found out all of the other gnome families were also involved in collecting box-tops by the hundreds to raise enough tops and tokens to responsibly pay for his entrance to this grand University of Gnomes.

University attendees follow the same scheduling concept as do human children and adults. There is a much longer winter break though, due to the amount of relatives visiting during this season. The village tends to be filled to overflowing with friends and family now down south for the winter holidays. So much so, that the boys have friends stay for sleepovers that extend for several weeks; the extra room is needed for the visitors back at the village.

Graduation at the University is on or around May 1st. Diplomas and certificates are highly appreciated, especially where details of their grades or accomplishment are noted. Successful completion warrants an 'A' or 'A+'. 'A++' denotes the highest form of achievement. These are marked plainly on their exams and report cards. Tests tend to be oratory by nature, so that all can learn from what the gnome, elf, leprechaun or faerie has learned. Our gnome boys and girls are expected to hold classes of their own for younger children, teaching the ways of humans. Curriculum includes, "Greeting the People", "The Way They Are," "Probing the Mind of Man – Without Instruments."

Gnome University™ was built in our garden and gnomes from all over the country, and some international guests too, have been our pleasure to host. It is fascinating to hear what they learn at school, and of their activities and their social interactions.

We were able to help out both the children and the elders. The children needed tuition and pocket money. The builders and elders needed construction materials. We provided the children a monthly allowance of a roll of pennies (at their suggestion) for school supplies and books and other things that kids "must have." As regards the construction requirements we made countless trips to the builder's store for pipes, and fittings, boards and fixtures. They even led us to a stack of beautiful red bricks they picked out for the foundation, and bought some for this requirement.

A PERSPECTIVE ON GNOME SCHOOLING

Children who are particularly gifted in one subject or another may take special classes to advance their natural talents, these take advantage of their gifts. Gnome children that demonstrate brilliance are given special opportunities not afforded others. They would not work in the gardens or do other more-physical labor, although they would love doing this. The clan recognizes and holds in great esteem a child's ability to make extraordinary achievements, which benefit the entire clan.

WE CAN SEE THOUGHT BUBBLES

> *"We'se educated 'cause we can see the thinkings of the people."*
>
> — Gnome Billy exclaims

"Peoples don' think straight, they have thought bubbles the elders tell us. Us educationals are the one's who can better put together the bubbles an' understand the peoples. Some peoples' thought bubbles are closer together, an' those are easier to understand. Some peoples' bubbles are even and consistent like a string of pearls an' those the people we'se work with the best. We just fill in the missing spaces so the human people make sense to us."

"The hard part is talking back to the people, 'cause we don't speak in bubbles too easily. So we talk verrrrry s-l-o-w-l-y in shorrrrrt sentences. Then use people can hear us better. This may be 'cause human peoples have limited eaahs."

"We'se go to school at the University so we can learn to talk crazy like human people. Eventually we work it out. We learn sub-jects like 'lectricity, an' 'puters, an' cooking, an' magic, an' spirits, an' directions, an' anger management (of people)."

The University is for Learning

DingleDorf, Grand Leprechaun Elder

"The little ones have got to learn that lesson number one is that they are here to learn. They can get so easily distracted, but this presents a problem. Everyone MUST pass each course at our institution; there are NO "C's to be had. We use a point system to regulate the school bodies, and there is time at certain intervals for those who are deficient, to make up the lessons. As each lesson is somewhat uniquely taught, this varying method provides a new and interesting opportunity for the students to catch up with their classmates."

"The University is particularly focused on helping Nature People cope in a world of humans. Our aim is to teach an understanding of the ways of Man and to help the Nature People develop their skills of communication and harmony with humans. This has to be done slowly and carefully in order to be effective, and so that humans can willingly learn to see the people of all the Nature realms."

VICTORIAN LADIES

PROPER LADIES

GIRLS LOVE SEWING

The girl earth nature people are drawn to pets, cooking and sewing. Much like the Victorian Dames of olde, the girls and ladies enjoy these daily tasks and view them as a cultural accomplishment.

Over the years we have observed a particular joy in the women when receiving squares of material from which clothes can be made. Gnomes are practical, so it can be a blessing to receive heavy flannel and goods for making nightgowns; be sure to add buttons. They are just as happy to have material and buttons to make clothes for the men and children, as for themselves.

The elder ladies take sheer delight in receiving silk and other fabrics with which to make special occasion clothing for those events. Shiny adornments are received with glee. We like to include gilt edgings, tassels and colorful threads, as well as sewing tools, in our gifts. Sometimes decorative beads or other ornaments are available in the stores for the holidays.

The ladies will always exhibit extra concern for the clothing of the young'ns. So consider their Victorian reserve and make sure mamma gets some nice material for her own special occasions. A soft green or creamy yellow will make a delightful summer dress. You can indulge their dreamy desires by gifting them with a satiny piece of material for a luxurious nightgown, which they can be proud of and very comfortable in too. You can feel their appreciation when they receive something they would never ask for themselves.

THE SEAMSTRESSES
Women folk make their garments by hand. Much about the gnome culture and activities is reflected in their clothing. However, it is the unspoken seamstresses, who outfit the entire clan so that they can be best prepared for the work they must do. In gnome society, these women are particularly appreciated, and often celebrated in special and memorable ways, whenever an opportunity arises. Most often, this is by way of gifts that have been traded for, or a special food ingredient.

It must best be noted here that the seamstresses are not necessarily the mothers, or mothers of their own children. They are a class of gnomes, and this is their work. They may sew for hundreds of gnomes, each. In this regard they are like their class friends, the teacher gnomes, who are also highly regarded by the clan.

SET OUT SEWING MATERIALS
Since gnome ladies and girls do a lot of sewing, they greatly

appreciate when you leave a spool of thread out for them to use. Sometimes at a dollar store, you can find prepackaged spools of thread of varying colors, with needles and maybe even a thimble, and small scissors, for a nominal price. A wonderful gift idea is to give the ladies your miniature sewing pack, which is complimentary gift that finer hotels provide. Such sewing kits make an especially excellent present during the holidays.

MEAL PREPARATION

The ladies gathered alongside us today as we did the final edit on this section. It is Sunday and they enjoy their traditional Sunday bake sale. We were urged to bring downstairs a fresh pound of home-made fudge, which we were inspired to get the day before yesterday. They have been munching along, hardly able to speak or comment on the previous sections as they are thoroughly enjoying the butter-rich fudge mounded with walnuts. As Christian reads the title, "*Meal Preparation,*" they exclaim, "Ohhh, here it comes!"

We laugh not knowing quite what they are referring to, but the very first sentence kind of says it all:

Women prepare the meals for the husband and children. Women usually have many children. Since the children take a great number of years before they reach adulthood, the mothers have a long span of taking care of the young'ns.

The ladies laugh themselves, holding large chunks of fudge, "There, see! We've gotta do all the work! Now maybe the world will see how hard it is to be a mamma, and we'll get the appreciation we deserve. An,' maybe some more of this delicious fudge."

We took a break and went outside to review with enjoyment the ladies participation in today's editing. Christian noticed one of the ladies lift her hand to slightly cover her mouth and share a comment to her friends, "You notice they didn't mention laundry?"

PET WATCHERS

Younger girls are devoted to watching over your pets when you are away. To this end they have not failed to help us. They will routinely stay and comfort your pet should you need to board them; this, so they can calm them and reduce their howling and stress. Girls can zap an animal to bring about a drowsy feeling should it be in the safe keeping of the pet. When the girls take care of your pets, they most often do this in groups, each with specific tasks. They take such responsibilities seriously and will maintain a constant vigil twenty-four hours a day. You WILL receive psychic affirmations about your pet's condition, comfort and safety regardless the distance.

In the many years that preceded this friendly relationship with the nature people, we authors have never known our pets to be so calm and healthy when they were picked up. Anyone with pets at home is encouraged to understand the loving nature people in your home and garden as well. They can bring warmth, health, happiness and comfort to animals and humans alike. We recommend that you be open to this special care that the girls can provide for your pet when you are away.

Pets are psychically sensitive to the energies around you. When you notice them especially excited, such energies may be too strong for them. We, as humans, naturally attract this anxious, stressful or negative energy, and it is not so good for us either. It can be worse, however, for our pets. Ask your gnome caretakers to work with your pet in such circumstances, the results can be instantaneous. We may be astute enough at these times to use a sage smudge stick around the house, over the open doors and about us, however, we often forget to surround the pets – which ought to be done first thing. Beyond this personal effort, the gnomes are caretakers you can place a lot of trust in, and reliance upon.

Gnomes have a natural connection to the Ætheric Plane,

and therefore the Ætheric Aura around us and our pets. This is very often referred to as the Health Aura as it represents the energy that we draw our health reserves from, the pranna. Though the gnomes can work with this energy around your pets to keep them well, they also have a particularly keen interest in doing the same for you. Ask for a little more vitality and a quick check-up the next time you hand over your pets to the care of the gnomes. You will both feel better for it.

A Ladies work is about dispensing Love

Mamma, Leprechaun (wife of Elder/Leader Peabody)

Momma says that, "Every girl should grow up to be a proper young lady. They can do this by baking love into every loaf of bread, putting warmth into each pair of pajamas you sew, and stitching comfort and security around every one of your lovely quilts."

Granny says knitting is a lost art. "Truth be known it is 'knot magic' of the oldest kind. We made things to last a long time, ages ago, especially our spells. By knitting our loving intentions into everything we made, we ensured healthy and happy lives for our young'ns, and this helped them to grow up to be loving people too."

GNOME GARDENING

WATERING

Gnomes get most of their water themselves from the ground or rainwater stored under it. Watering is a major activity of theirs as they are both nurturing the plant life, and stocking up for their own consumption. Gnomes require a lot of water, both personally to drink, and for their activities. For this reason they are very conscious of maintaining their clean stocks.

You will note the gnomes sudden disappearance during heavy rains. In addition to ensuring against flood damage, and other drainage issues, they are concerned with pure water collection.

It can not be over emphasized, gnomes need a lot of water personally. If you do house your gnomes, or travel, you must have plenty of bottled water on hand or very pure spring water. You will undoubtedly hear this yourself from an elder, perhaps subconsciously, but a message for sure.

SOIL MAINTENANCE

The first secret to growing and maintaining beautiful plants and flowers is the necessity of good soil. A rich organic soil greatly aids in water retention and as a long-term nutrient provider. A dump truck filled with a mound of dirt is appreciated. However, it does not provide the highest quality topsoil. Instead, check your local home store nursery for various varieties of organic topsoil.

Choose a variety that has natural content as part of the mix instead of one without. Natural soil is always preferred to chemical fertilizers when there is a choice. By introducing good quality topsoil, it is no longer necessary to dig into earth for soil, which would otherwise filled with roots and rocks. Gnomes will also love the fact that you will be mounding up the garden with wonderful rich earth that they can use for their farming, gardening, and truth be known, even trading.

By the way, whenever you see mounds or small hills they are usually a sign that gnomes are living there. Europeans are aware of this and know not to disturb such areas. They can be rather large cities and villages for many gnomes. The gentle folk of England, Scotland and Wales, who have a rich heritage of knowledge of the little people, magic, and the enchanting life all around, are familiar with these hills.

They realize that such may also be ancient burial grounds, which should be respected.

The good people of Ireland would never dream of disturbing the gnome hills. In a documented story about an airport runway expansion on that fair emerald island, union workers refused to flatten the area -- and after some time, the airport expansion had to use a different area for the growth.

Since you may need many bags of soil to fill your flower beds, do consider asking your home store or garden center to deliver your order, which hopefully includes bricks or stones to encircle the flower beds.

You will definitely want to avoid chemical sprays for minimizing outdoor weeds and pests. Pesticides and herbicides may resolve a pestilent or weed problem, but could as a result, poison the soil. This can make it very difficult to grow flowers in your garden for some time. Pest control products undermine the work of the gnomes, which is to bring in vibrant Universal energy to living things. Gnomes can help you by naturally warding off pesky insects or at least condition them to interact more harmoniously with the garden, the gnomes and you.

MAGICAL GARDENING

Your garden will be resplendent in magical properties when you have gnomes to help you. There is a feel, a color, and a light to your garden area which can not be translated into human words, it is an experience. You will hear the magic at work. The sounds of the earth are an inaudible orchestration of natural wonder, a symphony and synthesis of energy and intent. The earthly resonance touches us on a spiritual level making your garden, and yourself come alive together.

You can help the farmer and gardener gnomes by watering your garden, removing weeds, fertilizing and by adding rich compost-like soil. Remove any fallen branches and spent leaves, which represent unnecessary work for the gnomes.

Gnomes absolutely love gifts of seeds. They grow delicious vegetables in the lush patches that the "gifted" seeds produce. Being natural collectors, the gnomes will also store the seeds for later use as food and for trading with passers-by. They take pleasure in trading both flower seeds and herbs. Please note, the primary use of seeds is for farming, and not eating, though they can sometimes be seen snacking on seeds from their knapsacks.

The little gardeners take particular delight in dandelions,

roses, and marigolds, all of which have multiple purposes. Such variation of purpose is an inherent quality in plants, but these three are held to be particularly special.

Roses are used in their entirety in essential oils. These they put on candles for scent of magical fragrance, which wafts generously through their homes. They make for good food ingredients and have medicinal properties. Roses are prized for their magic; never is a fallen or dried leaf wasted.

Dandelions are used as a health elixir often in an infusion of tea. However, these may be consumed through the day as if chewing a straw. Rumor has it, that the dandelion milk can be fermented for the use in wine making – but we can't confirm this, or at least the elders won't.

Marigolds have magical properties and are used widely in practices from protection to manifestation. On the positive side, they bring good luck and prosperity to the human families of the gnomes. They also bring Good energy which can apply to health, relationships and justice. Marigolds are a "hot commodity" as pertains to trade and are often the actual gold amassed by both gnomes and leprechauns. Marigolds are a particularly thoughtful and purposeful gift for new brides. In that regard, they portent happiness, success and gifted children.

Marigolds create an exceptional positive energy force

around the gnome village, and therefore naturally protect them without any additional effort by the gnomes. Part of the magic of marigolds is that they can react to energy frequencies conceptually similar to an organic crystal. This has notable application in balancing of the Sacral Chakra and for healing the underlying organs.

The gnomes have a custom of placing marigolds on the eyes of the sleeping humans for whom they love to help make dreams come true. They also bring marigolds to their human families when they purchase or move into a new home. These they insist be placed at the northern quadrant of the property. The marigold attracts in nature those things that humans, animals and gnomes will find beneficial to their lives. For example, bees will produce the most glorious honey from these. The bees are drawn to marigolds because they have a healing effect on their senses.

The above is offered through the channeled advice of elf Carson. Carson is rather modest and was not seeking any credit but we thought it considerate to mention this fact here at the end. You see, nonetheless, that elves are great keepers of knowledge and have provided a delightful and insightful dissertation on magical gardening.

The Leprechauns can work their magic in your garden as well as elsewhere, and perhaps more so. It can be a veritable magic shop of ingredients, and the flora can be particularly splendid.

Here is what we recommend for the Leprechaun Garden

DingleDorf, Grand Leprechaun Elder

"The first thing to realize is that this is OUR garden area. We will take care of just about everything if you simply designate a special place for us to work our magic."

"We like the traditional 3 and 4 leaf clovers, of course, but have other interests as well. Marigolds will abound. 'Special' dandelion grass will grow in abundance for our personal concoctions, and for trading with the Elves. The Gnomes go tipsy for our particular species of Magic Mushrooms — they require a secret formulation known only to us. This is where they get their particularly useful properties. We require only your love, and some soil and plenty of water to work our enchantment in your garden. Everyone will enjoy the magic we bring forth."

THE LADIES PREPARE THE FESTIVAL

Festivals are a particularly joyous occasion that draws everyone of all ages. They provide fun, food, and merriment for the entire clan. Preparation for festivals often starts the day before, or sooner. Arrangements are made to receive and house many travelers. Dishes are cooked in advance too, and in sufficient quantities to feed the civilized hordes of visiting gnome families. Those that arrive the night before are greeted with a smile, given cozy beds, and treated to a warm meal featuring the local fare. Rest is important to the nature people so all are refreshed before the festival events begin at early morning.

The kids start off with play at the crack of dawn, looking for adventures on the nearby creek, roping from majestic trees, or tracking exotic birds that they had not chanced upon before. Gnomes like to hop and jump and run around in circles. They dart through openings in trees and under branches, hiding behind rocks, and leaping to see who can catch the highest branch. Since gnomes don't play as seriously as human kids do, they have just as much fun if they miss the branch and plop into the pond below — or go tumbling down the hillside. The latter happens a lot.

GNOME GAMES

All gnome children, and quite a few adults truth be told, like to play hide-and-seek. They play this particularly well, since they can pop-up to a branch twenty feet high, or slide under a nearby log pile in almost equal time. Hide-and-seek is a "sensing" game with them: Unlike the human counterpart, they use their astral perceptions to seek out their quarry. Although they have extraordinary fun tantalizing the animals, teasing humans that wander into their midst is also fair sport.

Gnomes like to play stone tossing too. Now mind you, they actually toss rounded pebbles, they do not throw stones in this game. Humans will detect such goings on when they hear things plunking into their beverages or feel restrained knocks to their heads. It is the "reaction" that the gnomes are trying to achieve. "I bet I can make him do this!"

Gnome kids are very adventurous and the more kids there are around, the greater the adventures. Festivals are a time when kids can be kids. This is when they climb the highest trees, slide down the watery troughs, shimmy up water wheels, and even attempt the more risky water rafting.

The gentlemen take off their vests during the day. They roll up their sleeves and partake in the manly game of "stone toss". At this event the neighboring clans can compete and show off their local champion. On more than one occasion they have happened to toss a gnome kiddy or two.

The girls have a game where they wrap nearly a hundred feet of either ribbon-like material, twine or vine around their waists. They then attach themselves to a tree by tying the vine. With great flourish and some eager help from the boys, they hurl themselves outwards and roll down the hillside competing for first place. Gnomes invented "fast women."

The girls have another fun game of collecting naturally colored eggs which they display in baskets at the festivity tables. Finding the rare specimens are the competition. These will be used the following morning for the parting community breakfast. They call the breakfast "Cottage Eggs". Lizards are never allowed at gnome festivities because they will eat the eggs. This is one way you can tell that a gnome festival is going on – when the lizards are conspicuously absent.

"Well Wishers" is another exciting game that everyone partakes in, even the elders. In this game, they fill an above-ground wishing well with water. They loop a chord from which a gnome will hang on to through the crosspiece. The crosspiece is tied to the leg of a nearby bird that the children must approach ever-so-silently. When everyone is ready the kids make an eagle sound, "Screeech!" When the bird flies away taking the crosspiece, the gnome gets dunked. This is an equalizing sport where the normal reverence for the elder is set aside, as it is done for any adult. Everyone gets dunked to the delight and joy of all.

Those that are completely dunked get to make a wish, which everyone else helps to make come true. Their wishes, though, are practical ones like getting the first piece of "corny bread," which is a mixture of corn kernels smashed, dusted with flour, and deep fried, ... or four gnomes grabbing the arms and legs of an elder and carrying him up the hill for dinner so he does not have to walk, ... or horsy rides for the kids on the Statesman of the clan.

Gnomes have a game called "Hot Bottom" where they see who can sit on the peppermint leaf the longest. If the contest is close, they douse the leaf, and kid, with water to intensify the effects. "We think this is where the humans get the expression 'cool,'" they say.

Marbles is another fun activity for the children during the festivals that can occupy hours of their time. These are organized as vast contests of challenging teams in varying age groups where skills are demonstrated with successively larger marbles. Although similar to the human counterpart in this sport, it is more participatory; a gnome kiddy has to be sitting on the marble. The team that knocks off the most gnomes wins. This is the sport that creates the most noise, so if you are listening, you'll know when the festivities are well underway. They save this game until late afternoon. When the children play they are always supervised by an adult for their protection and safety.

These games, foods and concepts are copyright © 2006, the authors.

FESTIVAL FOODS

Some of the festival activities are delicious. One luscious event entails tapping tree sap and letting it drip into the mouths of the children who take turns partaking of this natural treat. Honey combs are also gathered rather carefully and used to dip twigs into for chewing on throughout the day. "Bark baking" is an early activity that provides a hearty afternoon treat for the children. The bark is from trees ripe with sap which crisp up into a caramelly flavor. This satisfies a child's hunger until the feast. The supervisors always ensure that all the children have a healthy drink of water between each activity.

While the gnome boys are playing marbles, the girls' last activity is to see who can build the largest pine-cone tree. The activity requires them to climb the cone petals and lift up the successive pine cones. These petaled cones were selected after giving up their pine nuts in preparation for later delights, like Pine Nut pudding.

As the day wanes, the children have to take their afternoon naps. This is a must! The men begin their card games, tile games and chitter-chatter, while the cooking goes on and the long tables are set. When the gong goes off, the children need no encouraging as they fly from their cots and temporary tree hammocks salivating with anticipation for the feast that they know awaits. Gnome children are allowed to grab their portions first at this kind of festivity, so that they are not underfoot or cranky while the adults partake.

FESTIVAL ENTERTAINMENT

The gnome children eat together in the children's area under the guidance of the caretaker, who not only oversees the children, but also orchestrates an almost endless venue of acts and entertainment. One of these events will be the magic show, as this is a never-ending source of amazement for gnome children. And almost as certainly, the well disguised magician is the clan leader who finally lets his hair down to play with the children. Gnomes like bursts of light, things turning into birds, and prankish tricks like instant rain clouds over just them. The gnome elder has a mesmerizing effect over fire-flies and can awaken and control them to perform dazzling coordinated effects.

Most festivals are not complete without a visiting contingent of marching elf flutists. After the excitement and thrill of the initial scores, the elf flutes play synchronized and dispersed sounds to recreate perfectly the moods and events of Nature. From peace and serenity of an early morning dawn, to the chilling effects of a midnight thunderstorm the stories are told to the sound of music. "The Pipes" is always the long anticipated performance. This is an instrument of varying sized, tube-like flutes tied together. The elves are said to have the ability to re-create any emotion, and dramatic stories can be told through this music alone.

"We come together in the Mountains."

Peabody, Leprechaun Elder/Leader

"There are grand forks and ancient trail ways where all paths lead to the festivities. These roads are well hewn from centuries of wagon wheels hauling barrels of grog and loads of wares and produce indigenous to the travelers' lands. These are all gifts to the local Leprechaun leader who is expected to first sample the offerings and then to make the choice of how the exotic fare is to be prepared. He chooses dishes from distant memories, which help make the occasions all the more special for all."

THE FESTIVAL FEAST

At the gnome community meal, the women do not serve the men. It is a family style set-up. Out of respect, the women are seated first with the men holding out the chairs until they are comfortably situated and the passing of the fruit begins. The gnomes start their celebration meal by collectively enjoying the local fruit harvest. The food, in this case, is actually placed on the tables so everyone reaches for that which pleases his or her pallet and enjoys the evening at leisure.

FESITIVALS ARE FOR CELEBRATING

What happens next can vary from event to event. Sometimes it's a coronation, other times it's a holiday, yet another might be a seasonal celebration (such as a solstice or select full moons.) Sometimes, it is merely the joining of clans and receiving of visiting delegations of almost any earth Nature People type.

Another reason for these festivities is to coordinate the gnomes' moments of family and unity with those times that their human hosts are in high spirits and likewise enjoying holidays and special moments. The gnomes will celebrate your good times and your good news along with you by holding festivals.

OTHER GNOME ACTIVITIES

BASIC SCHOOLING

The gnome teachers conduct their classes irrespective of age. From youngsters to adulthood in some cases, the gnomes participate together in the subject of the day. Classes, however, are not taught as a contiguous course of study, but rather, the curriculum is varied to support the current interests, situations, and necessities of the clan. Therefore, subjects are often repeated and represent current and updated material with each dissertation.

Gnomes do have designated teachers and these are often the women. Children in particular perform their routine studies as these are required by the gnomes. Beyond this, and yet rather frequently, gnome adults participate in the training process by providing enlightenment and training on their individual specialties. Instruction with the adults often includes field trips and participation in the actual activities under study.

Gnome schooling may tend towards early morning instruction. They have been observed leaving for school in groups early in the morning. Schooling can continue until naptime. Sometime on very rare occasions their instruction continues after the naps until about 6PM. During summer or times of extreme heat, the gnomes have been observed and heard to have the day off from school. You may find yourself being urged to attend an afternoon movie or drawn to satisfy a sudden urge for ice-cream. They have also been known to take long breaks from schooling for practical considerations.

Both the boys and the girls participate in schooling, which is where multiple programs can be introduced. For example, many of the girls will participate in sewing instruction for the entire day. Boys, however, may be off observing bird migration.

"Existential Dentistry"

Smurrf, Blue Faerie

"I am a prize student. There are not many Blue Faeries that go to the University. I am privileged. I am learning Existential Dentistry so I can be of service to the Man kinds. I am learning to make the teeths grow healthy and happy so the peoples don' have to give them up. We'se been collecting them for years, now, and know all about people teeth. We can't afford any more teeth so now we'se going to help you learn how to keep them longer and make them grow better. Cavities actually start with a subtle mental condition, which is where my specialty field can make a big difference."

MUSIC

Music instruction at Gnome University™ is not a frivolous endeavor. A grand piano has been procured for instance at great expense. So much so that it is not easily purchased again for other locales to which the gnomes may move. Violin, and chestnut cups (banged together) making a clang sound, and other lessons are given. Perhaps these help in support of their opera productions with their most talented singers.

They have a type of wind instrument in which they blow over enclosed strands of spider-web. It produces a very high vibrational sound that is a softer tone than the harp, with the notes lasting longer. Gnomes have a hand held instrument which is a rack comprised of infinitesimally small metal bells which produces notes beyond the perception of human ears (very high.) It's like the sound of descending angels or twinkling light and is often used for dramatic effect.

They also have a water instrument where chambers hold different capacities and issue forth percussion sounds. This is analogous to a drum; however, the tone is more natural and plays upon the emotions. For example MMMMMMMMMMMMMMMMM may signify silence, or another tone may mean someone like a deity (perhaps Ghob) is approaching, or the sound of a pallor pouring over things. It has a deep resonance. These notes have a correlation to our OM sound.

Gnome music is complete unto itself, usually conveying a meaning, message or story, and as such does not require vocals. Conversely, they do have singing, which is so well intoned and melodious that it does not require instrumentation to enhance it. For example, when young gnome Chester sings, the quality is so angelic and the tone so pure that it resonates, providing its own background. A human would find it completely captivating.

Though we have not heard any of the operas as yet, they do have such productions. One of the gnome mothers is herself a great operatic diva.

He speaks about his mother:

— Peter-Jön

"First of all, we don' calls our people divas, 'cause those are angels. We call dem songsters or songsteresses, which would be like song-stars an' song-star-esses in humans'es words. Songsteresses awr owr special people which you'se peoples would call 'Specialty' people, I think."

"Songsteresses can'se just become a specialty people because they'se got talent. Our songsteresses have to first be able to do any of the udder things that any of the udder gnomes can do. Then they'se have to be fully educated, not just 'bout the gnomes, but 'bout the udder nature people too. This is 'cause the songsteresses are ambassadors too, and they represent us in all the places that we let them go. They make the impressions for us. An' der music is 'spose to be part of the message."

"Although most gnomes stay in der clan, the songsters an' songsteresses have to also travel for part of der education to learn the rest of the world or else they won' be able to have relationships with the udder peoples [nature spirits] there. When they understand the peoples from the other places too, then they come back to their clans an' der music is developed."

"Gnome music is something that is developed with the help of the elders because it must tell stories that they want said and be ac'r'ate but not offensible to the udder peoples out there, who can be very pec-u-liar. My mommy for real is a songsteress and I had to miss her a lot when they sent her away on the journeys. But they say, 'cause she was so smart, it's why I'm smart now an' get to enjoy priv-e-le-ges like living with my human people family an' go to the University."

"Yes, we gnomes have operas 'cause owr music tells stories. When Mommy sings, she is not 'spose to just sing the words, she's 'spose to make you feel about where she is, where she's singing 'bout and the peoples in the story, an' all the stuffs that they're doing. Songsteresses go with our real Ambassadors when we meet new peoples, an' they are the one's that tell the new peoples who we are through the songs. Then they feel good 'bout us an' we can do trade things with them."

"Mommy can sing other songs too, like children's stories, and dems the one's that I hearded the most. When I was just an itty-bitty gnome, no bigger than an acorn, she would sing me stories all 'bout nature. She would sing 'bout the birds that woke up very early in the morning, an' 'bout all the animals that came out to play during the day. Her songs would sing 'bout all the kiddies getting up for breakfast an' the yummy berries an' fruit they were getting to eat, an' how all the gnomes would go off an' do so many mah-velous magical things in the world. Each thing they did could be it's own song."

"She had songs that ex-pres-sed the moon coming out at night an' all the warm cuddly moments that the gnomes'es families had - cuddled up in der homes. An' she even sang songs about the gnomes'es telling us bed time stories. I always liked, she said, the stories she sang 'bout the human peoples in the world. Sometimes they were happy, sometimes they were sad, but I liked the adventure one's."

"When I was growing up, an' I asked Mommy questions, like "What makes flowers grow?', or 'How come they're purple or pink?', she would sing me a song an' I could learn things that way. I'se learned a lot of things, but I can'se sing as nicely as she can or as Chester can. He's got glorious voices. But dat's OK 'cause my peoples Daddy takes me everywhere anyway. An,' 'I'm a different kind of Ambassador,' he says."

"Human peoples can sort of hear the gnomes singing

but they'se only getting some pieces of it' cause der eaahs are too short. Dat's such a shame. Cause then we could just sing you owr songs, an' you would know all about us too."

He directs this next comment to us: "OK you can clap now!", to which we enthusiastically do.

BUILDING A BETTER WORLD

Gnomes are industrious nature people. They can often be seen filling their days performing necessary construction and repair. They do these things joyously and as community effort projects. Everyone works on the homes and the buildings or on the water channels and dams without thought to individual interests. Each is constructed with personal loving care and reflects varieties of styles and attention to function.

Although a delightful gnome home may seem a little off kilter, it probably reflects the most effective use of some natural element such as a convenient tree trunk, or mountain side out-cropping. To take advantage of the opportune shortcuts that nature provides, their architecture might appear rounded, tilted, or in disproportion. Regardless, their homes and buildings are particularly solid and long lasting and provide coziness, warmth, ease of access, and proper air flow.

REPAIRS

Upkeep is an important part of the day. Almost without thought the gnomes routinely tend to the repairs of all their construction works. If the first thing that catches the eye of a group of gnomes is a roof that is beginning to sink, then they will immediately turn their attention to that project for the day. They tend to work from their central clan location starting with housing and spread outwards as time permits attending to the needs of their structures. They don't hold the thoughts of "Do I need to do any repairs today?", but rather, "What shall we repair today?"

FENCE BUILDING AND MENDING

One repair that requires frequent attention is fence building and mending. Gnomes are an organized sort, and fences serve a variety of purposes. Beyond the natural division of homestead — farming and protection from outside sources is accomplished by endless constructs of functional, but oft time peculiar looking, fencing. They like stone walls the best because it is naturally pleasing to them and has durability. Stone walls provide additional benefits, things only gnomes would think about. They are natural and durable pathways. They are also fortification. Stone walls provide greater stability against inclement weather. They better block debris and intrusions from the physical world like farm animals.

PIPE FITTING

Pipe fitting almost seems like a hobby or fun interest to the gnomes, as they exhibit a special fascination for pipes, fittings, and fixings of all sorts. Sometimes the endless windings and meanderings of tubes and pipes and angles and bends seem to represent some construction of art, although I'm [Christian speaking] sure they would argue 'natural' benefit. When questioned, they may say it's for strength, or reflects the materials on hand, but one can not help but sense the enjoyment they take in using as much of such material as may be available.

The gnomes exhibit a natural curiosity for the complex and seemingly endless mazes they work with. When I've tried to recommend certain "shortcuts," the gnomes retort with a critique on the advantages of gravity regardless the excess lengths and twists, Christian recalls. "Ahh. So what if we have to make a couple dozen extra trips to the home building store so they can shop around." I can recall a similar captivation with erector sets, Legos™ and log cabin games. To tell you the truth, I wait with anticipation myself to see if these contraptions will really work.

THE SOCIAL GNOME

Gnomes are community-orientated beings. They host gnomes who are traveling to hot nourishing meals, and warm beds - sometimes for a night or for many, many years. Environmental conditions may require such lengthy stays. Within a village hundreds of gnomes or more work together to build a wonderfully peaceful and productive community.

Tasks are delineated based on one's proclivities and abilities, from farming, and building, to cooking and cleaning. Children help out in almost all aspects while still spending time in between for their learning. The teachers are quite adept at developing many skills essential to gnome living while still recognizing a child's special talents, abilities and inclination. Gnomes are community beings who work, play and enjoy frequent naps in your plants and trees. Together they exist in clans.

EXCHANGE AND TRADE

GNOME CURRENCY

Gnomes have no conventional system of currency or taxation excepting gold, gems and "coppers" and nickels, which they are fond of (for the metal value) for use as passage. They work by means of an arrangement consisting almost entirely of trade. They trade with other gnome clans in the neighborhood, states, territories or provinces and also with visiting gnomes from across the country and globe. Of particular note, they trade with leprechauns with whom they enjoy mutual respect, and with whom they make exchanges for magical things such as the opening of doors to buildings, rooms, and cars.

GNOMES HAVE PROCLIVITIES

We have found that the gnomes' proclivity for mimicry of human behavior in the family has resulted in observable use of coins, paper money and credit cards, peculiar as the latter may seem. Our value attributed to coins is not understood by them. Paper money constitutes a means of equal trade more than a trade of specific value. You will find your young gnomes willingly standing by for you to put their goods on your credit card while you are checking out. They will carefully pack and stack Ætheric copies of toys, candies, special foods they enjoy, baby clothes and tennis shoes in your cart.

The gnomes are naturally polite and will either suggestively nudge you to look at something of particular interest, or ask if they can make a purchase. They would be overjoyed, however, if you purchase them select <u>physical</u> items like those described above because you thought of it. Such helps them become more "a part of the physical world". These are their whimsical ways and demonstrate their fascination with humans.

They will eat the Ætheric counterpart of the candy, play with the physical toys, and wear the baby clothes and shoes. (You will probably find that the clothes, shoes and jewelry you are inspired to buy them uncannily fit their stuffed bear perfectly.)

Like other behavior of the human family, the gnomes will try and imitate them so as to share and fit-in with the family. When given the indication that they are part of the family, the will quite literally participate in shopping.

Coinage is an intriguing and valuable commodity to the gnome. Indeed, they favor shiny pennies, which they call coppers. In addition to pennies, they like nickels. (As I am typing this, my little gnome assistant here is saying they like what a nickel is made of, meaning they value the composition of the coin.)

Earth nature people do trade with coins for certain purposes. For example, they keep a coin in their knapsack should there be difficulties along the journey. They can use these to barter assistance from other nature people, or for passage — a tradition in many earth-based nature spirit kingdoms.

HOW TO INCREASE THE GNOME STANDING IN THE COMMUNITY

Tending your garden, such as by planting flowers, not only increases the value of your property, but also increases the gnome village's standing in the community. The gnomes are able to fetch a better price for their goods from traveling gnomes when their village is surrounded by beautiful trees and shrubs, and of course flowers.

If you have had problems growing flowers in the past there are a few secrets described earlier in the book, which you can follow that will help you. Your flowers will flourish. Your gnomes benefit as well, as the soil is already enriched, thus requiring less labor from the wee folk.

"Gnomeses basically like to share."

— Gnome Chester

GNOME EXCHANGE IS A FORM OF SHARING

"We exchange and trade things with the thought that we are sharing the wonderful things that we have with other gnomes and peoples, and they share their wonderful things with us. We understand the humans call this 'an exchange' or a trade. But really, we are all just sharing with each otha the results of the work that we each do. This is how everybody helps to take care of everyone else. It's true that when we give something to another, or share as we call it, we would expect them to share something too."

WHY MONEY IS SELDOM USED BY THE GNOMES

"Money is not really used because we're not trying to buy something where there is no exchange. Since money has no value, gnomes don't think of it as something to exchange, or trade with. Of course if the money is made of nice copper and pure nickel than that has value to us an' we can use the piece of copper metal or nickel metal

to trade with. The numbers you put on the metal doesn't make sense to us, but we do know how important copper is an' nickel is. Although you don't hear about it much, silver is important too because it has special properties. We keep that in the caves in the treasury boxes so we can use the silver for us. Silver can make things clean an' we use it for medical steps too. The high wizards sometimes use it for reflecting purposes. This can be with open light, but it can also be used to reflect the light that's inside of me and you. (Christian is wondering if this relates to self scrying.)"

GNOMES TRADE FROM THE HEART

"Trading is a word we like because it doesn't exactly mean equal. Gnomes trade from the heart. We trade something that has certain 'portance to us, and the other gnomes, elves or leprechauns would trade something of similar 'portance. If elves don't have any salt, for example, then salt would be of 'portance.

WHAT HUMANS WANT TO EXHANGE MOST IS LOVE

"With people, you kinda people, we try to trade with

love, 'cause that's what you want most. You think you want udder things, an we try to trade those things too. We try to make it a feeling or experience though, an' not so much the money or the trip or the new bicycle. When we trade with humans it's difficult 'cause they want to see things their way. So, in that case, we help 'bring things about' as the elders call it. This way they experience the things in their world. Peoples wouldn't fit on our bikes, an' they don't see the love in getting a basket of onions."

"What people give us is a kind of love that they don't know what to do with, so it's 'free love' as the elders call it. This means we're allowed to trade for all the free love that the peoples have. The peoples, you'se peoples, give us places to live, an' help us with the gardens, an' bring us building supplies, an' bottle up water for us, an let us play with their little kids' toys."

GNOMES CANNOT TRADE FOR TOYS

"The elders don't let us trade [with] the people for their little kids' toys. We don't know why, but we'se told that we can just play with them when the other kids are playing. I think their saying that the toys are personal,

and that peoples, you'se peoples, don't share and trade personal things. Personal things [belong] to you. The elders say we can't understand the 'iportance of things belonging to humans, so we just try to know what those things are."

GNOMES SPEAK ABOUT PERSONAL POSSESSIONS

Christian was trying to explore this concept of personal possessions with Chester. Since we know there are things that they hold out as being as their own, or would otherwise like for themselves, we have a contradictory understanding that we would like to clarify.

"Personal things to gnomes are those things that identify them in a unique way..."

— Chester says

"... so they exemplify (we had to help him with this word) the unique characteristics of the gnome. For exzample, I like things that are yellow because that sound is natural to me, and it makes me feel bettah. It makes me feel healty. SO I like yellow clothes, yellow gems an' rocks, an' other things that sound like yellow to me (musical notes or vibrations that resonate similarly to the color yellow.) Yahh!, for egzample, I like the letter arrh

[R]. Chest-arrh! See!"

"That resonates to yellow," Chris asks?

"Yah! Your name is the same as mine."
— Chester says

"Christoph-arrh. Chest-arrh! See there Mommy you re-ginate with me too!

"Ahhh. Yes sweetheart," Christopher says warmly. "You're right!"

GNOMES NEVER TRADE IN PEOPLE OR ANIMALS

"Gnomes nevah trade people an' animals, 'cause that's against the laws. An' you can't do that because people an' animals aren't really ours to trade. Udder peoples an' animals are already sharing with us by being here."

"Saturday's are the biggest day for trading. This is because the human people aren't in the way too much, an they sleep in real late that day, an human people don't want to work on that day, so we make that our big day. Human peoples like to go out and do different things an' go to different places that day so we let them haul

our stuff, and set up shop where evah we end up. But we usually know where their going anyway, an' maybe sometimes we're suggestible (meaning they put thoughts in your mind). Gnome kids like little doggies, they're like good little people. They [puppies and dogs] think in complete sentences an' not thoughts of bubbles [like humans]. So we can understand them."

GNOMES LEAVE A LITTLE SOMETHING

"When we go different places to trade, or when the human people take us to different places, we do leave coins for the passage. That is something that is expected, and it is a courteousness. We pay respect to the local gnomes an people that welcome us by bringing them a coin or small gift, but in that case we're not really trading, we ahr being considerable."

At the same moment when Chester said, "Does Mommy want to ask a new question?", Chris started posing one.

DO GNOMES HAGGLE?

"Is it true that gnomes have day-long or many-days-long negotiating sessions regarding a trade, with much intense haggling, or similar exchange?"

"Aggh ahhhh aumm aummm (clears his throat for a while). OK! I'm getting something, ummmm ... Here is how that could be true, Mommy, although it wouldn't be so complicated as you say. You see, what you is talking 'bout, is when the really big an' 'portant elders are trying to work out an immensible trade between clans, not indivisible gnomes or lit'l groups. 'Cause the elders are act-u-ally negotiating for all the gnomes in their clan, there's lots of things to take into 'sideration. 'Cause each gnome or family might need different things. So the eldahs have to try an' satisfy the bunches of needs or find something 'portant enough to everyone that they all want to share that."

IT IS EASIER TO TRADE BIG THINGS

"It act-u-ally easier when gnome clans are trading for very big things than when we are trading with the elf clan or the leprechaun clan, an ohh my gosh, the troll clan. Yikes! An' the brownies can be verrry tricky. An' the bush people can be verrrry stubborn. An' we can't always understand where the fairies are coming from, so we get puzzled from them."

"That was my next question," says Christopher.

GNOMES ARE ABLE TO WORK OUT DIFFERENCE OF OPINION

"But this is what I think you want to know. Nature people can work these things out. We don't run away in huffies, because it's most important of all, that everyone get along. 'Cause we all have to live an work together so we'se got to be 'telligent an' learn sometimes what to trade an' how much an' when an' where an' with whom. The gnomes are always respectable of all the udder peoples an' we know we just have to find the s'lution that fits everybodies needs. Is that negotiation Mommy?"

"Yes – absolutely", says Christopher.

"Cause we nevah beat up people."

KNAPSACKS

INTRODUCING GNOME KLONDIKE

Christian (at the start of a session): I'm getting Klondike wants to speak. Let me take a break and tune into him first.

Klondike, one of our newest mountain gnomes nervously takes note he is up.

> **"I've never dun public speaking bee-fore."**
> — Gnome Klondike says

Christian teasingly and good-humouredly replies. "We'll that's no excuse. You're the star of the show today. Greatness is your middle name!"

Klondike is a newer member of our family, and he is a mountain gnome. He joined us close to the time we were doing the final edit on the book. He's a little larger and stockier than the other gnomes. We knew of him because he interjected a comment in the middle of a conversation the previous week while driving, and Christopher asked, "Who said that?" Christian picked-up it was a little gnome child who went by the name Klondike. Visually he has patches of brown and blond hair which is kind of bushy.

Christopher comments: "The other nature people children say he is stubborn, but very well mannered. They said he hogs all the attention and likes to be the star. In writing this I was amazed that Christian started by announcing Klondike would be the star of the show today. How curious that the kids had only just told us of his proclivity to be the center of attention only a week or so prior."

In truth, Klondike's persona is more akin to "there is but one right way to do things", which stems from his family's role and responsibility of "gatekeeper" to the community. Gnomes take their roles as doormen (to homes, or buildings) and gatekeepers (to major road entrances) very seriously and act with the highest professionalism and care.

"Daddy ... I only know about back-packs in the mountains."

— Klondike says

"We call them *knapsacks*. I have a backpack now 'cause you bought my tuition, but most of us kids in the mountains use the knapsacks. Daddy, I think I'm shy."

Christopher: "Ahhhhhh."

Christian says: "That's OK. You just have to think what you want to say to me. Speak like your just talking to me, in my mind like you usually do. I'll worry about writing it for the book. You don't have to be nervous about writing, just tell me your story."

> **"OK, I'll bet it'll be a good story too!"**
> — Klondike says

THAT USED TO BE A SECRET

"The reason we use the knapsacks is 'cause we can carry them with sticks. Now here's the really interesting part. Our sticks are very special. We hand pick a straight branch that we think will hold up for a long time. We carve directions to the places were going to go - in a circle around the branch. Each circle of directions is for a different place. That use to be a secret ... hahhaha. Now, the older kids have longer sticks 'cause they have more places they have to carve into the stick."

WATERPROOF BACKPACKS

"We make our knapsack with big square pieces of beavah [beaver] skin. 'Why', you must be asking? 'Cause — they's watah-proof. We fold up the four corners around our goodies an' tie a knot to put the stick through. More about the knap sack to follow…"

Christian: "Ohh... he's becoming a ham now."

Christopher: "No, this is excellent writing (to Klondike)!"

GNOMES VALUE BEAVER SKIN

  "I wanted to hone in on beavah skin for a moment an' elucidate on its special value to us. You see, 'Mr. Know it All,' [referring to Christian] it behooves us gnomeses to enter the forest silently. We do this thusly. We wrap beavah skin around our feet or boots for three reasons. Firstly, its watah proof right? Hahaha. Good for crossing creeks, an' crawling through the damp thickets an' underbrush. We tie them on our legs with leather straps, but you probably figured that out already."

"Elucidate? Behooves? Thusly? I think you guys are being coached," Christian queries.

"Your doing great Klondike," Christopher informs the little one, wanting them to feel comfortable talking openly.

  "I sure they like it." "You think their intelligent enough to get it?"

GNOMES TRAVEL UNDETECTED

  "The second reason we where the beavahs on our feet, is so's we can walk quietly. When we steps on the branches and leaves, it muffles the crunchy sound. Then we can silently approach deers an' burds. This is a great way to get the best eggs, an' no one even knows ... hahhaha. Sometimes we even have to sneak up on the bears, 'cause

they hoard all the best goodies, an' take it back to their cave. Sometimes they take our stuff, an' we have to go get it back, ... an' we leave them just the bare necessitates. HAAAAAAAAAAAAAAA, I made a funny!"

FOOT POWDER

"But the bestest reason of all to weah beavahs on your feet is so they don't stink. If the animals smell our stinking feet, they'll know the gnomes are comin' an' they'll hide their eggs and feathahs [feathers] an' things. Also, it's the only way we can sneak up on the elves. 'Cause their reluctant to communicate with us an' will just move on unless we just walk into their camp an' say 'Hey! Feed us!' 'Tell us a story.' 'What do you want to trade us for the eggs?' All the creatures of the forest know what beavahs smell like. So they just think beavahs are walkin by looking for wood."

ROPE LADDERS

"Befores we go anywhere, we verify that situation is safe. In our mountain knapsacks we carry a little rope climber. This is about six feet of rope. In the middle, for about one foot is the main part. We tie a small loop above and below this foot. Then we find the straightest, tallest tree, an' loosley tie the two open ends around it. We put ah feet in the bottom loop an' ah hands in the

top loop an' shimmy up the tree. We can't goes anywheres if we see smoke."

THE KNOCKER

"We also use ah sticks as knockers an' udah things. We can knock on the trees to signal the udah kids. We can use them to see how deep the watah is. Sometimes if we'se in trouble, we can create diversions by knocking on the trees making the birds fly up. This is why our sticks have a big knocker on the end [knob]. We use 'em to knock the honeycombs off the trees an' get the yumyum sticky honey... Sluurrrrp. We have to eat the honey right then though, 'cause if we try to bring the honey home, the buzzy bees will just follow us. Sometimes we use 'em to smash nuts. But you can't hit 'em too hard."

"Got anything else Klondike," asks Christopher during a pause, who was already thouroughly impressed with all the knowledge imparted?"

We were talking about knapsacks," Christian reminds Klondike.

"You said you were going to return to the knapsack later," Christopher states.

"Ohhhh Yaahhhhh."

"'Cause the knapsacks are watah proof, we can fold 'em like cups an use 'em to drink watah. By making cups in ah hands we can catch fish too. But only the little one's. Sometimes, we tie the wet knapsacks on our heads to keep us cool. We also can use them for pillows."

"Gnomes like marbles. Even us mountain gnomes carry a couple of marbles in our favorite knapsacks. Pieces of apple are really good too. 'Cause you can eat them, an' you can share 'em with the animals. Animals can smell apples. We carry one stone that's sharp for carving things."

GNOMES WORK WITH THE MOOSE

"We have mooses an elks in the mountains. So you gotta carry treats for the mooses an' the elks. The mooses an' the elks will let you ride in their horns if you give 'em treats. They know all the best trails, an' can travel real far. An' nobody messes with the mooses."

"When we's visiting udah tribes, it's best to come in riding mooses an' elks, 'cause you look very important. This is a big gift too cause the mooses can move things an' carry things for the tribes. The mooses also help the peoples get the highest nuts an' berries an' leaves, an' sometimes birds nests for the best soup. Some of the real mountain gnomes make their bird nest soups with the eggs still in the nest. But we don't do that, 'cause we'se civilized."

Christopher sharing: "Give him some more brownies."

Klondike: "Yummies. It's got chocolate mountains in it. [Chocolate chips in the brownie]"

"Best part about the mooses an' the elks, is they take us ovah the hills. Gnomes don't like to climb mountains [if they don't have to]. That's too much work. Mooses do it all day long. So it's no trouble. But you have to promise 'em something when you get to the udah side."

"Mooses will always take you to where the watah is. So you don't have to worry about that. Then when you wanta come home, you just float down the stream by making rafts out of your knapsacks an' sticks an' rope."

THE GNOME UTILITY BAG

"The biggest reason we'se carry knapsacks is 'cause we don't know how long were going to be away, an' what we're going to encounter on our walk. We might encounter unfriendly animals, difficult terrain, an' even unfriendly an' difficult forest people. (He looks down. He seems to be reading from a script.) But forest people all *have their price. Pref-er-bably, we can give 'em nuts an' berries we find along the way for passage. But sometimes they want our apples, an' that's not so good. The ohhhhlllld ones want a coin, so we have to be prepared. Fortunatley, we find coins along the trails that we take. 'Specially where evah humans go fishing an' camping. We take the worms off the hooks for 'em, an' take a coin in trade."*

Christopher: "Why do they take the worms off the hooks?"

Christian: "They do it because they think the humans want the worms off the hooks – that they are caught – so they take them off to stop the suffering of the worms."

Klodike continues: "When the people don't have any coins, we take their marshmallows instead. 'Cause every-body in the mountains likes marshmallow ... that's guar-anteed passage - 'specially with the kids; they'll let you get by an' show you the way."

DON'T TOSS EMPTY SODAS

"We try to roll the cans an' the bottles that we find in the mountains down the hills so they collect along side the road for people to pick up. But it takes 'em a long time. I don't know why. I think they're worth five pennies. We would rather the people just left us the coins, 'cause we can't trade cans. Peoples throws us the cans

back out their windows instead. I guess they'se don't want the five pennies."

GNOMES CARRY ROOTS

"The udah good thing about knapsacks is that they can hold all the different barks that we pick up along the way, an' the roots. This is part of why we are taking the journey to begin with — to bring back the medicines an' the healing woods that the old cranky women gnomes use to make the magical elixirs."

"Wasser-Sisser tells us that this is why we are so short. 'Cause of all those funny concoctions they feed us. Haaaaaa. They keep saying, 'Take a little of this — an' a little of that' . . . an' we all ended up being little. So there are little people everwherah, but they sure ah healthy. We think it doesn't work on noses though. They keep getting biggah. So granma keeps pinchin our noses when she gives us the medicine, so the noses stop growing so big."

Christian: I think I know what he's talking about. When you took medicine years ago you held your nose, so you don't taste it — or smell it!"

"Hee-hee-hee."

ೞ PART – V ೪

TAKING CARE OF YOUR GNOMES

ACCOMODATING THE GNOMES

PEOPLE CAN MAKE HOMES FOR GNOMES

Little gnome Everette wants to say some things. He is slightly pale, has soft green eyes and the biggest curly mop of red hair you ever did see. Most people probably wouldn't even notice his slightly pointed ears.

"Hi!"

— Gnome Everette

"Are all those trees [logs] in the trucks that we'se see's driving by from our mountain being used to build birdhouses?" (We've noticed these trucks when land is being cleared to build new homes for humans. We think Everette's concept that this wood is being used to help the animals in nature is a beautiful thing, and TRY and believe it ourselves.)

Everette has one other question though. "Who's going to hang up all of those birdhouses?" Christian conveys to him that, "All the people probably just hang up one or two each, and eventually all the houses get put up."

Christian notices that young Jacob, a little medical student from our Gnome University™ is fidgeting.

"Hi Jacob! Do you want to say something?"

> **"Hi Daddy, I am nerve us."**
> — Gnome Dr. Jacob

(They had settled on calling Christian "Daddy" after a long time, while figuring out what the naming should be.)

"Don't be nervous. You said you wanted to talk today [This is the first time he has ever spoken for this book.] And today we're talking about manifesting. Did you want to talk a little about that?"

> *"Ahh Huh."*

Jacob stretches and plays with his long ears a bit. He is a bit rotund for a child, but we've long since helped him overcome his image complex. He has started talking very openly and knowledgeably about things he has learned at school. Soon, the words flow freely.

> **"Peoples gives us Gnomes hope that we can have a better life too."**
> — Gnome Dr. Jacob

"This seems to be in answer to the questions on our

minds [of how to help gnomes and nature people] when putting together the book. They pick up on these thoughts as a counterpart to telepathy."

"When peopl'es do the right thing, they make our lives better. When they clean'se the grounds, we can move 'round easier. When they put up 'dem fences, they can keep away the hungry animals that eat all of our grass'es - and let 'dem go to their own grocery yards. When peopl'es don' burn so much, then we can breathe better too."

"Peopl'es can make things. This is goodness. When they make us'es homes, an' little shovels, an' little benches for their kids and dolls, we can use 'dem too. We really can!"

"When they make the wadders go to all the right places then more of us'es nature peoples can live in more places too. This is ver'wy ver'wy important 'cause wadder is ver'wy important to us'es. If you'se tak'es the wadder away, then we don' have any wadder eider. An' the birds don' come. An' the birds help us'es a lot in our lives."

PEOPLE CAN SHARE THE FOOD THEY GROW

"When peopl'es grow the foods in the ground we can enjoy 'dem too. But we not stingy or greedy. We just tak'es some that we need. If you'se don' use the pesticides, then we can help those plants an' vegetables grow good and strong — so'se der is enough for you'se peopl'es and us peopl'es — an' it has all the best stuff in 'dem."

"Gnomes work very hard on helping plants and flowers to be healt'y and strong. They would not be without us. An' the faeries help too. An' so do other nature peoples. We make 'dem smell good, taste good, be healt'y and vibrant. An' you'se peoples need all of these things."

"But we need you'se to plant 'dem, an' water 'dem, an' help bring in the minerals an' nutritionals too. We have to work togedder as a team. An' I want to be your leader. HAAAAAAAAAAAA!!! Was I funny daddy?"

"Yes! Very good funny Jacob," Christian replied as Christopher laughed.

RECOGNIZING WHEN THINGS ARE GOOD FOR YOU

"Things that are good for peoples sound good. There is music that comes from everything and you'se can know what sounds good and bad. You'se should eat the things that sound good, do the things that sound good, an' be good you'se self."

"The music is in you'se mind and it tells you'se truth about things. Do the things that sound good — an' you'se doing good for everybody and everything too. This good music is important part of making all things healt'y, 'cause without the music you'se, an' I, an' everything is like a plant that does not get wadder."

BE PREPARED

EARNING THEIR MERIT BADGES

"Gnomes really don't have nurses."

— Rudabegah is talking

GNOMES CAN TAKE CARE OF THEMSELVES

"We are all actually trained to take care of ourselves an uddahs. We believe in preventa-tive medicine, an' preventi-tave measures. For sample: We don't venture out all alone. We are always with at least one uddah who is familiar with our destination an' how to get there."

"Our partners know an' understand us an' what we need to be healthy an' vigorous. This is why were always in two's. We can counter-balance each uddah. If one is tall an' able to get the leaves on a tree, the uddah one is short an' can gather roots. If one has bad teeth, then the uddah one is good at pulling them out."

"We don't go anywhere without knowing first where we're going, an' what we expect to encounter along the way, without checking the conditions as best we can or without permission from the elders. They make sure we

have everything we need in our knapsacks, an' they tell us what to say to the uddah nature people who we will meet on our travels."

GNOMES ARE BROADLY TRAINED

"We are especially trained-up on all circumstances. For sample: If we're going to have to live on fish, then we learn to be good fisherman first. We learn how to use everything in the forest in all the ways it can be used. These may be for function, for food, an' for heal'th. Gnomes believe everything has at least three purposes. If it don't, it's a waste."

GNOMES MAKE MAPS

"Gnomes like to make maps of the places they go to, so we don't walk around in circles so much. The elders painstakingly develop rotes [routes] an' make relations with nature people along those rotes. If we'se spose' to go through Bush People country, then the elders will usually pack for us things were spose' to bring them as we go through their territory. Bush people like cinnamon sticks. They don't eat it an' use it for heal'th like we do. They like to smoke it, 'cause it smokes for a verrry long time, an' makes them feel good."

"If we're spose' to bring back stuff, that's liquid like,

then we plan our journey through lands with tall reeds an' rushes so we can hollow out the long tubes an' use them as storage containers to bring back the special 'grediants. It's easy to drag along reeds filled with 'grediants that are biggah than we are."

GNOMES CONSERVE ENERGY

"We don't like to waste any movements. If we don't have anything to do, we would rather just stay still an' take a nap 'till some'in comes up. We don't take things to any place, where we don't have something to bring back. Even when we go somewhere to play, we take something we can trade with the other kids. That way we eventually ALL get to play with the best toys."

Christian: "Sort of circulate the toys."

GNOMES KNOW CONDITIONS BEFOREHAND

"Sometimes, the weather isn't so good. But you aren't a very smart gnome if you don't know what the possibilities are before you go, an' make sure you have everything you need in your knapsacks an' backpacks, an' a few extra things too."

"Sometimes we meet up with a gnome who has gotten lost, an' he's walking around in circles. These are the hopeless ones. We'se spose to take them along with us, so

they learn new things to help them in the future. Then we drop them off along a fitting trail at our earliest opportunity."

THERE ARE THREE PATHS

"Now here's a big secret: THERE ALSO has to be three ways of getting anywhere. We don't venture out until we understand these possibilities, an' are prepared for each of them, 'cause you nevah know ..."

GNOMES ARE PREPARED TO CAMP OUT

"Gnomes have to be prepared for the 'ventuality of having to stay in a strange place overnight. Your hats have to have a little blanket in them, an' a snack to hold you through the night. If you get home early, then you can have the snack anyway. If you weah a scarf like I do, then you can make a hammock to sleep in, or a tent."

"If it's a long journey that you're going on with several friends, then you should let your hair grow. You can cut it along the way to make a nice pillow, an' you guys can take turns sleeping on it. Do you realize how important it is to have a comfortable pillow and a warm blanket when you're all alone in the forest? This is why you have to be prepared. It might take you forty years to get home. I'm not sure, I can't count yet."

GNOMES SEND WORD AHEAD

"Many times messages are sent ahead of time along the way for peoples to expect you. That way you can drop in an' have a warm cozy place to sleep, an' food for your belly. You don't have to trade for these things, 'cause it's arranged for in advance by the eldahs."

"Oft-times the travels are [in order] to take messages. It's one of ah most important activities, an' it's how the whole forest knows what's going on. People are going back an' forth all the time, so sometimes you hand off supplies or messages along the way. So things can get to their various destinations that way. The most important message is when the next festival is going to be, how to get there, an' what you might want to consider bringing as a gift. Just a suggestion mind you."

GNOMES OFFER GIFTS

"Sometimes, the eldahs send stories and songs an' words of wisdom as gifts, or for trade. These are very well received. An' certain eldahs develop great respect for this reason. It is a great privilege to meet the eldahs of another clan. So, one wants to learn the particular likings that they have so they're prepared with a proper gift or exchange."

GNOME GUIDES AND CHAPERONES

Should gnome children accompany you on long distance travel, adult gnomes will come along too for the children's protection. They are usually gruff worker gnomes with a more burly body as evidenced by their muscles, and are usually in the prime of their life. They often do not say very much, as they take their role as gnome bodyguards seriously.

GNOMES LEAVE NO MAN BEHIND

In an emergency, gnomes can quickly make a stretcher out of twine bark and branches to carry the injured. When there is need for help, adults can put out a special loud cry to alert nearby gnomes. This cry is a piercing one and can be useful for warding off an assailant. They can also send psychic messages for help to those humans that are attuned to them.

AN EARLY EXPERIENCE

— Christopher

"We were traveling in California just prior to beginning this book. It was before we knew we could formally invite the gnomes to travel with us. We knew they were traveling by foot to the same destination. They were heading up to Carmel from our last stop in Laguna Beach. It hadn't occurred to us to invite them to journey with us in the car."

"What was interesting, was that we had originally planned a stop in Santa Barbara that day, but had to give up the excursion due to time constraints. Coincidentally, it was near Santa Barbara where Peter-Jön twisted his ankle and fell. He fell as he was young and he was trying to keep up with the 'protector' gnomes and elders in their rapid trek to reach Carmel, our designated rendezvous."

"We were similarly pressured to make good time, and found ourselves missing our highway exit and traversing hundreds of miles deep into the California canyons. Our frustration carried us late into the night and into a remote one-stop town. We were on fumes when we reached the village truck stop, which was but a moment from closing. To our dismay the sole pump was not even working."

"We had called upon Archangel Metatron for help, just before finding this quasi-oasis. An angelic woman at the truck stop received us warmly. After hearing our plight, she gave us directions to a working gas station in the next town. She called ahead to see if they were still open. The angel let them know we would soon be there. It wasn't long before we came upon this divinely manifested gas station in the middle of no-where."

"As we coasted into the gas station, Christian heard that loud gnome cry (described above) and picked-up on a desperate psychic message, 'Daddy, Daddy I broke my foot. Come and get me! The gnomes are dragging me in a stretcher and we're hungry.'"

"Christian sent back an immediate message, 'Peter-Jön where are you? I'll come and get you. Stay where you are!' Christian asked where Peter-Jön was and got that he was still some distance from Santa Barbara. We were able to get gas in those few moments before closing, and cross-country directions back to Santa Barbara. We headed out at lightening speed. We called upon Archangel Metatron once more again to help find our injured child. Intermittently, Peter-Jön's psychic messages continued. He exclaimed, 'I can feel you coming!' For the first time that day, we actually felt good about the journey."

"Travel difficulties continued though, as we overshot the rendezvous point that Peter-Jön had communicated. We then sent the message, 'We are very close to Santa Barbara.

Can you carry the stretcher a little further and meet us there?' They said, 'We have a way.'"

"Soon afterwards messages came in, 'Daddy. I'm riding the water balloons.' Christian began picking up on King Neptune of the sea aiding the endeavor, and began figuring out that the gnomes were now traveling on porpoise."

"We were all guided to a lit-up pier, sparkling invitingly under the full moon over Santa Barbara. In the exuberance that followed, we were able to quickly piece together the events of their amazing journey and understood that synchronistically, we all ended up where we were supposed to be. We also realized that for the rest of the trip all the gnomes could just ride with us in the car."

"I did an energy healing right there along the pier. Peter-Jön could hobble now - if you could imagine a gnome that normally hobbles, now hobbling with an injury. I called on St. Mark and St Luke, and the Archangels Metatron, Uriel, and Raphael, to bring Peter-Jön healing energy through me. When Peter-Jön was healed a huge Ætheric butterfly appeared fluttering about the wide-eyed patient. So as to sustain our relief, we decided to forgo the night's journey to Carmel, and returned to the original plan of staying overnight in Santa Barbara."

"Peter-Jön must have been better, because he remembered

he was very hungry. It was moments until 11PM and we spent the next half –hour looking for some place, any place, that was still open. We happened upon a pizza parlor along the coast and upon entering they told us, 'We are just closing.' Christian pleaded and said, 'We will eat standing up and don't need parmesan," convincing them to make a five-minute pizza."

"Peter-Jön noticed the large racing video game near our table complete with a car seat and steering wheel – a gnome's dream   We fed it quarters and enjoyed his exuberance as he got to experience driving for the first time. His exhilaration seemed to overcome his hunger, for it was hard to entice him to stop long enough to have a slice of pizza. It was only a bite or two later when he remembered his most favorite thing in life was cheese."

EVER WARY OF THE WEATHER

During severe rainstorms there is the need for gnomes to work in rubber boots. Having to toil in harsh weather conditions is necessary when it downpours for several days in a row. Rain is a concern as it can cause flooding of the gnomes' underground cities and homes. During these anxious times the elders play a central role. They call the clan to action, including the young'ns. Underground dams must be fortified, channels are checked and various structural improvements are made to ensure the water is safely diverted.

Looking like coastal fishermen in bright yellow slickers and floppy rain hats, the little ones are expected to help out in any way they can. They really get into the spirit of the effort. Some are in charge of gathering twigs that are used to bolster the dam. Others carry out excess water with sand box pales. Always the clan works together perfectly achieving unity. This harmonious clan response typifies the team spirit of the gnomes.

WATER

GNOMES PLACE ATTENTION ON WATER

Christopher

"I wanted to know why they bring up the need for water so often. This subject has been introduced by them frequently when we discuss food, trips, sleeping and health. I presume it to be an essential aspect of their life and have myself emphasized it in my writings."

Christian

"Little Carson, our shy elf, says he wants to do one (answer a question). So, my view of synchronicity is that nothing is by chance. I would like to hear little elf Carson's perspective on why gnomes, and presumably all nature people, place a strong emphasis on water."

"I've got my braveries today."

— Elf Carson

"Elves are the one's who keep track in records an' books of the information for all the nature peoples. It is only natural that an elf answer these questions, 'cause they're much to hard for gnomes. AHHHHHahhhhh. OK."

WHY NATURE PEOPLE NEED WATER

"Nature people need watah 'cause --- do you know Mommy? --- You should know ... OK. I'll tell you. Watah is how the nature people become heaviah an' connect-ted with your place. Watah is easy for us to take in an' it has all of the element stuff in it. [Particles from all the minerals] Watah is the best way for connections to the different places [planes]. Watah has the best energy in matter for us right now. Long time ago we needed to be more with the E'art an' the rocks directly. Latah on we gonna need more air, like the fairies do. It has to do with owr convolution [involution], like Daddy says. Is that too hard for you to understand? (He was seriously asking.) This is why we tell the peoples you gotta drink more watah so's you can sees an' feel us bettah too."

Christopher drinks some water and offers some to Carson. Christian asks Christopher, "Did you know he was just asking for a drink of water telepathically to me? The water is helping him connect with us right now." Carson continues his inform.

"We like to drink watah tru straws. The gnomes say that's why we so tall an' thin. But actuality we normally get owr watah through the grasses an' the reeds an' the roots an' things. Gnomes drink it from the watah cups

that the leaves make. The reason the watah has to be good is 'cause we get the min-rals an' el'ments from the watah. The toxics make owr eyes go blind an owr equa-lib-riums spin. We fall ovah. This makes the fairies very upset. They'se [Fairies] always 'lecturing at people. Fair-ies aren' afraid of people."

Needs hug and asks if he's doing well – Christian and I tell him he's doing great, excellent.

"They always telling you peoples what you should be doin' right. Elves don' do that. 'Cause we'se just victums. When you'se burn down owr houses in the trees, we don' get mad. We just cry an' move along"

As mentioned earlier, both Brighton and Carson were rescued from forest fires in Florida. We took in many hundreds of elves and found them homes in trees nearby.

"There's not so many elves left anymore, 'cause the less trees there are, the less places there are for us. We can't do plants to well 'cause they're not tall enough for us. Daddy lets us stay in the house with the gnomes. An' that's great! We use the drawers sometimes an' the cur-tails (curtains to sleep in vertically) an' the pillows an' the pillow boxes [couches] when the dogs don't need 'dem."

"We can go to the re-frig-er-ator any time we want. An' we can get watah, an' celery, an' carrots, an' soggy lettuce an' PICKLES — yum yum yum. We like pickles! Daddy gives us toothpicks an' packaged sticks [wooden skewers] 'cause we don' use forks to well. Owr mouths aren' huge like the gnomes. AHHHHahhhhh. We learned to eat marsh-a-mellows. 'Dem sticky good. An' they made for sticks. I forgot what I was talking about Daddy?" "We we're talking about water, Carson," Christian says. Carson goes on: "OH oh oh. Elves like to go in the watah too. Gnomes go in little streams up to their knee knuckles. But we can really swim. Watah is good for the nature peoples' skin. It gets the 'purities off an' it makes owr surface more healt'y. The gnomes say this is why we look green. Ahhah. But we don' look green, we just always in the bushes. Elves can drink watah from the rain too. 'Cause it rolls down the trees into collectibles."

"When we'se done with the oranges, we let the halves dry out — an' we makes cups an' bowls out of 'em. Then we don' have to destroy anything. We don' know how to make plastics or rubber-ware. But they sure hold watah good. The re-frig-er-ator keeps it really cold at Daddys' house an' he keeps pops [naturally flavored soda pop] in dar too. It's like owr sap drinks. Chris'a-pher thinks we *shouldn' drink the pops but elves have naturally purfect teeth 'cause there's properties in the tree parts we eat that keep dem healt'y. Elves like watah'melon too. But they'se so heavy, we gots to share dem with the gnomes, 'cause they'se the only ones that can pick em up an roll em an' break 'em open. If you open a watah-melon, you'se spose to eat da whooole thing. That's why it's good to share too. The watah that we'se all drink is why it's easiah for peoples to see the nature people on full moons. They think it's their magic words, but it's the moon doin' it. It's pullin the watah to owr surfaces (body surfaces) an' we're easier to see. This is why we hide more durin' the full moon."*

After a pause: "Are you done," Christian asks?

   "Daddy I'm z'austed. I nevah talked that much before. Can we go play now?"

Christopher says, "Yes, of course angel. You did a remarkable job!"

Christian says, "I didn't know you were so exhausted. You guys can go play with the other boys and here is some more water."

GNOMES ARE QUITE RESILIENT

Christopher

"You may worry, as did I at first, that you may inadvertently hurt the gnomes through an unintentional move or action. I was frequently fretful about shutting the door before they all were through, or, accidentally sitting on them. They are not always, or even usually, visible. Please set aside these worries as the gnomes are quite resilient."

Christian

"The dimension of time that gnomes function in is different than ours. This keeps them safe. Gnomes are naturally able to move faster in their time, rendering our movements slow. They can do this selectively, and specifically for the timing advantage. Furthermore, through such means, they can avoid accidents. Gnomes can be likened to large air pillows rather than the fragile eggshells we may imagine them as."

Christopher

"This brings to mind the time the kids consoled me, saying that they are like cartoon characters that pop out after a mishap. Now they are telling me:"

> ### "We go plop!"
> — The collective gnomes

"That when we get runnded ovah by the big Acme truck, we go plop! Then slowly our hats come out of the plop, and we stretch an' pick ourselves up out of the plop. Poof — we are perfect again."

By keeping themselves "light" gnomes are less affected by what happens in the physical world. Their lightness is what constitutes their invisibility. In effect, they have taken on but little of our heavy physical world matter. Nature spirits have the ability to use both Ætheric matter for their composition as well as astral matter, which is even lighter.

The particles of matter which make up the Ætheric are vastly spread apart. Therefore their matter seldom comes in contact with physical matter from our world. Their Ætheric matter is like electrons in comparison to our world of large molecules, with quite a difference in size and density. Thus, gnomes are better able to prevent most accidents in our world than are we.

Do invite your gnomes to hold on to your clothes or body when crossing a busy street, or ask them to be especially light in an area where there is much activity and movement. Although they may land softly, or bounce as on the moon with little gravity, or simply blend into our matter like water on sand, your mental anguish must be considered. They DO feel your discomfort.

JACOB IS STUDYING TO BE A DOCTOR

"I's study'n to be a doctor for us gnomes. We don' cut open each udder EHMMMMMmm! We do it from the inside by bringing in the things that we need to be healt'y. We live to be ver'wy ver'wy ver'wy old. Older than you'se peoples by many many times ... 'cause I's such a good doctor ... HAAAAAAAAAAAA!!!"

"If you'se peoples knew how everything worked in you'se bodies, an' why you'se needed certain things from the ground an' the plants - things that we put there - you'se could be old too like Dr. Jacob. I's not really a doctor HAAAAAAAAAAAA!!! I's just a kid, but I'se learn'n to do the doctor stuff, 'cause that is what I's 'spose to do in my life."

GNOMES CAN GET SICK TOO

"Peoples don' seem to know that nature peoples can get sick too. We don' get sick 'zactly the way you'se do, but we are not just the most healt'y sometimes. Some of the things that you'se peoples do are what make us unhealt'y. The burning forest, an' no wadder, an' no land are big problems. We need certain things from you'se peoples *places to build off of too. Pollutants and things in the air and wadder can affect us. Also lots, lots of sun is important."*

"The 'nergies that you'se bodies create are helpful to us. When you'se are healt'y you'se create healt'y 'nergy 'round you'se. We need that healt'y 'nergy too. Give us some. HAAAAAAAAAAAA!!! The way you'se peoples feels — the happier and healt'ier that you'se are helps produce better 'nergy 'round you'se bodies. I an' other gnomes like me an' other nature peoples too are working all the time to help make you'se stronger peoples. But you'se are stronger then we are so you'se have to help you'se self too."

GIFTING THE GNOME

One experience, which is sure to delight your house and garden gnomes, as much as you, is "Presents!" Gnomes just adore receiving gifts of all kinds, for any occasion and for one and all. Gnomes are not selfish. They would be as excited if a friend got a gift, as he or she would be if it was received personally.

They see gifts as a form of appreciation from humans, and a desire to better understand and relate. However, it cannot escape notice that some gifts bring particular joy and excitement. Such gifts may be available for ordering at www.thegnomesdepot.com or your local stores.

NATURE

CRYSTALS and ROCKS
We have found that gnomes like to go to the crystal store and rock shops with you. It's a magical place filled with energy vibrations and glittering treasure they resonate to. They like to hop from rock pile to rock pile investigating all the different stones and crystals. They handle the stones, listen to the crystals and find that special one they resonate with.

They see the different colors and feel the unique energy in

every rock and crystal. Your gnomes may become enamored with a colorful rhodochrosite. They may sense the awesome power in quartz crystal. Gnomes will marvel at the balancing potential of kyanite. They stare endlessly at the age-old fossils encapsulated in rich amber.

Their hands buzz as they lift giant scoops of enormous topazes of every color. They hug the colorful stalagmites of awesome amethyst geodes. They lay restfully in a therapeutic pose across large aqua-marines, and spin endlessly on the magnetic poles of hematite. Their demeanor takes on the ever increasing hum of the vast assortments of crystals as they become directly attuned to the minerals of their dominion.

As gnomes are great collectors they will surely find two or three pieces each that they would like you to consider for their ever-growing collection at home. We now have many display boxes featuring their special assortments.

Ever since we took them gem mining at the local mountain tourist attractions, they've wanted their own rock tumbling toy. We hear it running sometimes for weeks on end while we are working around the house and remember the great fun they had, sifting through the silt and mud over the water flume for prized treasures. We know they will be thrilled at the brilliance and luster of the finely tumbled stones when the cycle is complete.

The gnomes picked up certain flat and sparkly stones along the trails recently and indicated these could be worn as badges granting safe passage through the mountains surrounding our encampment. They like stones of all kinds and are not necessarily taken in by the glitz and color that appeal to humans. Their greatest appreciation is for the intrinsic value in each and every priceless treasure of earth.

THERAPEUTIC WATER FALLS

Gnomes like things similar to human preferences for good energy, a small therapeutic fountain for one. A waterfall in their garden will really be appreciated for its aesthetic beauty and for its healing vibrations for physical, mental and spiritual health. These benefits can also be derived from water bubbling up and trickling down stone tiers with smooth creek bed pebbles scattered about naturally.

These wonderful little fountains can be inexpensively acquired at home and bath shops. Some come with submerged lighting in the water that adds sparkling delight and color therapy in the evenings for you and your gnome clan. You may decide to buy a second one for your bedroom, since water that is moving is as therapeutic as it is protective.

Tiered fountains and inset pools with trickling waterfalls for the patio area are also beneficial. They can be enjoyed for their aesthetic beauty. Like the in-house models, they are naturally protective and cleansing of the surrounding area since their waters are also flowing. Their natural charm can be appreciated by nature people of all types.

Often these pools are used as wishing wells and it is fun to give your nature family a "copper" (penny) now and then for their wishes. Let them hear yours verbally, as well as psychically, for the nature peoples' good-intentioned nature can lead to the removal of the barriers we place before our desires.

The nature people's abilities range from manifestation, through inspiration to psychic influence. Much of the magic that happens in our lives is through the natural expression of the nature people around us. They are not wish granters, per se, but they do want happiness, harmony, health and prosperity for you. Your involvement with them is the "action" that makes the magic happen.

While we're speaking of wishing wells, you should know that leprechauns are the most capable of direct manifestation. Their reluctance, however, is legendary. History shows more accounts of the innocents, such as children, and most often the girls, as benefactors of their gifts.

Leprechauns tend to adopt a human or family. Their presence is first marked (to get your attention) by the mysterious disappearance of objects which suddenly re-appear a week later. If you are so adopted it is an indication that you have an "arrangement". They get a place that they can call home, and where they can work on their all-important tinkering.

They feel it is important, and their responsibility, to fix broken things in the house, garden, and to repair faxes and computers. They want you to benefit from the family arrangement. When you first notice things disappear, you should start by inviting (mentally and/or verbally) the leprechauns into your home. If the objects re-appear, you now know you can complete the arrangement and will have leprechauns in the family.

Leprechauns are equally good at finding things for you. Write out a note, verbalize vocally, or communicate telepathically your desire to find something very specific. Then let the thought go and allow one day to one week for the recovery. It will happen. Just don't put too much hope on seeing leprechauns at first, as they take quite a long while before they trust any human in this regard.

Our suggestion for your relationship with your leprechaun is not to wait for a pot of gold to appear. Instead, find a gold bracelet or chain that you no longer wear, or similarly, a gold ring – perhaps from childhood – and tuck it in the spot you sense they like to reside. And, also plant some three or four-leaf clover. Gift them first! All nature people like to reciprocate, leprechauns especially. However, the gift they give back may not be material; they can truly make your greatest wish come true. Leprechauns can unlock doors physically, or as easily find opportunities in your life to make a difference by fixing or finding you a new computer, car, sewing machine or appliance.

MAGIC

WAX AMBIANCE

Candles can be used to give some outdoor lighting for the night-time goings-on or festivities. Votive candleholders can look like small bonfires for the gnomes. Candles attract salamanders (fire nature spirits), as well, and naturally set the stage for magic. Scented candles can add an irresistible inducement, encouraging the gnomes to enjoy the evening. Specialty candles like coffee, cinnamon and apple, butter-crème, and vanilla-hazelnut scents are tremendously popular with nature people. Baking scents in candles like sugar cookie, banana nut bread, cookie dough, and pumpkin pie will have your gnomes (and probably you) swooning in delight.

"The magic is in your Mind."

— Peabody, Leprechaun Elder/Leader

"Magic is not something that people do well when connecting with the Nature People. They would be better at this if they simply tried to be connected with Nature when they try to reach us. Your mind focus [mind set] is what is important and the better you are able to comprehend what we are, the better you will be able to reach us. I will go into this more difficult subject on our subsequent book of Nature Spirit magic." (See Book 3, [The Magic of Gnomes and Leprechauns … It's Natural]."

"When I was I wee lad, I used to wonder at all the marvels me Dad could perform. He told me, 'One Day, Peabody, you too will be able to do great things. This is because 'you believe.' That is the real magic behind our marvels, and a little bit of this, and dash of that. But these things will come.' Don't rush off to change the world just yet; it is a very magical place all on its own. First see the magic that is already there, and only tweak what needs perfecting now and then."

OUTSIDE ACTIVITIES

PREPARING THE GNOME FESTIVAL

Gnomes love a good festival and love to have a chance to celebrate along with you on holidays and at special occasions in your back yard, your deck, patio or indoors. If it is the Fourth of July, they would love to have a barbeque poolside with you or a wonderful picnic in the park.

Homey potato salad, buttery corn on the cob, sweet baked beans, raw celery, raw carrots, and a small portion of your main dish will be very much appreciated. Don't forget to give them some water. Clean pure spring water or rainwater is their preferred choice. Fruit juice flavored slushies are also a delectable treat for the young ones. They like that the frozen fruit juices freeze to their tongues and slowly dissolve into effervescent ecstasy.

To a great extent, it is the experience of festivals that they are enjoying most. Gnomes do not actually eat the physical foods that we do, however, there is an Ætheric counterpart which they can enjoy. This counterpart surrounds all matter and it is the main reason why what we do in our world, or plane, affects the nature people.

Gnomes do not consume or experience the preservatives in our foods, to quite the extreme as do we. Nor do they get ill in the same ways or for similar reasons. This is because earth nature people are of Ætheric matter, not our physical matter. However, they do recognize such impurities and avoid the Ætheric experience of them.

Experience takes another form as well, a psychic one. The gnomes feel the enjoyment you have at get-togethers and events, and it is that part they want to enjoy most. All earth nature people have a natural affinity for the fun of things. They are essentially spiritual children at any age. In most cases you need to perceive them as 6-11 year olds (though even the children can be incredibly bright and witty). The elders and leaders will come across more mature – but then again they may be a thousand thousands of years old in their years.

THE ART OF FESTIVAL DECORATING

Decorations are an important part of any gnome celebration. A few ribbons placed in the bushes and trees of their area will signify the occasion. Red, white and blue ribbons for an Independence Day celebration perhaps (or your pertinent colors). Yellow, green, and purple streamers can be hung around the garden and inside the home for spring holidays or special religious days.

Keep in mind that each nature spirit type prefers a different style of plant or tree. For example, elves will prefer thin, straight and narrow trees, bushes or bamboo like plants, and require water nearby. Leprechauns like cool thick-leaved areas where they can hide and blend into the greenery better, and hang out their hammocks for their late night camaraderie and dreaming. Bush people like bushes and tall bushy trees.

Gnomes like lower trees and bushes, but with cleared earth beneath them as they tend to be the gardeners who are clearing the lands of debris, and the ones who tend the soil and crops. However, gnomes are playful adventurers, so interesting tall or gnarly trees to climb are great fun for them, as are fences and bridges with water that moves under them or through large pipes.

Faeries are quite varied both in appearance, their nature, size and preferences. They like cleanliness, color and purity generally, so flowering trees without pesticides work well. Some like the tops of pines, as does our Blue Faerie who prefers blue spruce. Others are small, and like areas under steps and sills, so low plants appeal more.

Colored lights of all colors strung through the plants and branches of the trees of their associated outdoor areas also add greatly to the magical ambiance of the festival evenings. You may find the miniature colored and white twinkling lights stay up permanently in your private garden area, especially when they are on an auto-timer to come on at dusk and turn off after 6-8 hours.

The color of the lighting is important too, as preferences vary with nature people. Faeries like pale colors of the pink, yellow, blue and green varieties of miniature outdoor lights. These can be strung in the trees and plants where flowers are. Hang their gossamer ribbons and reflective buttons and bobs here too.

Leprechauns are pretty much rich green and gold colored-light lovers, and are more nocturnal, than other nature people. However, some fairies are also nocturnal. So, you can leave the lights on a little longer for them.

Gnomes like bright green and red in combination as this is an indigenous color for them. They resonate to these energy vibrations. Multi-color miniature lights also enjoyed draped around their mini-fences made of curved wire.

Elves prefer green lights and white ones that twinkle. Similarly, all-white is very good for working with Angels, although they are fond of soft pastel colors like the faeries. Bush people like darker greens and browns, so they are more difficult to attract with lights, but are naturally attracted to the plants themselves.

Bright reds, oranges, yellows in combination, are best associated with fire nature spirits, the Salamanders. It should be understood that it is the conscious spiritual essence of an Element that you are appealing to, not the element itself. This is true for all elements and nature people. In this particular case, candle flames actually work best as this element has a more action. They are the epitome of magical influence.

The Cloud Nature Spirit is the highest form of nature spirit on this plane, and the most evolved nature spirit consciousness therein. In the higher Mental Plane, resides the ultimate nature spirit consciousness, the Sylph which directly precedes the angel phylum. Although outdoor white lights, and mixed blue shades work well, these forms of cloud nature spirit consciousness are actually best realized in daylight; of course, a few clouds in the sky helps. These nature spirits do not demonstrate the playfulness of the other nature people, and convey more prophetic messages through their heightened state of consciousness.

Getting more down to earth, we return to the gnomes, elves, leprechauns, bush people and some faeries. These are happiness-oriented, fun-loving people that can instill their practice of play in you. Include them in your celebrations and feel the joy and harmony that they represent. Lights, balloons, ribbons, scents are all pleasing to them and call to their playful natures. For additional lists of festival planning and gift ideas please visit www.thegnomesdepot.com.

FOOD

THERE ARE BEVERAGES, AND THERE ARE BEVERAGES

Strong coffee is actually a particular favorite of gnomes. Younger children, though, may only be allowed to have the foamed crème on top of your latte's and cappuccinos. Teas are very popular too, but they tend to prefer ones of the herbal types, such as dandelion and rose hip. The properties in still other herb teas are well appreciated, even sought after by the gnomes.

Where cinnamon is used, the gnomes prefer the entire stick, as this is chewed. Gnomes have a more pronounced chewing nature than do humans, as you will observe from the various barks, reeds and nuts they like to snack on. Although milk is enjoyed, (all dairy products, frankly), they have a particular fondness for the milks that come from certain grasses and plants.

If you can help the women folk prepare their own soups and stews by giving them ingredients they can use in their big kettles, you will have their great appreciation. Remember, gnomes love spice. Moreover, (being 'earth' nature people) they like vegetables that grow underground in the earth for their stews like potatoes, carrots, turnips, rutabagas, parsnips, and beets. Adding above ground foods like squashes, zucchini, garlic and onions enhance the texture and flavor of the homey gnome potage. Gnomes tend to make big pots of food as the sole dinner item that is enjoyed by the entire clan.

Though the men may ask you for grog, do not worry if you must refuse to procure them beer for health or other personal considerations (we do not encourage the use of alcohol in humans). They have undoubtedly brewed their own from potatoes, grains or dandelions, which they will dip into if none is volunteered. As with leprechauns, their Ætheric nature actually benefits from these fermentations. Their experience is not so exactly compared with human inebriation; earth nature people function quite well after tall, cool, frothy pewter mug of ale. I wouldn't suggest such an offering to your faeries, however; honey ("slightly warmed" they say) and drizzled on a tiny cup of milk is much more to their liking.

Some cooking brandy in a small refined glass may also suffice for giving to your gnomes and leprechauns should you have some. Even the ladies will partake in this if it is somewhat diluted. Of course, should you decide to buy them bottles of fine European lager, you will have their immediate gratitude.

Try opening one bottle per festival, or weekly on a Friday or Saturday night and keep the rest of the bottles fresh for them in the refrigerator. Offering the open bottle, or perhaps some poured in smaller bowls or cups for dipping their mugs into, can be done in the early evening around 6 P.M. - or as the sun sets. Gnomes and leprechauns are enthusiastic for beer in the aluminum cans as well. They refer to these (especially the larger cans) as kegs. One "keg" can last from Friday evening well through Saturday night. Come Sunday morning you can pour out the physical beer (remember they have thoroughly enjoyed the Ætheric counterpart) and dispose of (or recycle) the bottle or can.

Areas which you feel have, or are welcoming to, leprechauns is a great location to set out the open bottle. You can split the serving into another container when you are also putting some out for the gnomes. (We now put out one bottle or "keg" and ask that the nature people share.) Grog is of great benefit to leprechauns - health wise and can help them in their magic making as it puts them in a slightly different state for such endeavors (so they say!)

TOYS

TRAIN SETS

Nothing will bring greater joy to gnomes, children and adults alike, than your gift of a realistic model train set, the more authentic the better. Gnomes appreciate quality and the real look and feel of the metal, details, and quality construction as opposed to a plastic toy train with no moving parts. Their sincere gratitude will endear you to them and them to you.

A real locomotive, carriage car, and caboose on a round track to start are sufficient. This can bring them endless delight as they fill their afternoon hours with play and role-play. You will see them in striped engineer suits with caps. You can hear the "Woo-Woo!" of the locomotive as it rounds each turn. Delicious scents waft from the travel car, and the young conductors call out at each station, "Allll A'Board!"

The carriage car can be important because it allows all the kids to ride inside. (Remember, they can alter their size to be smaller.) Therein the conductor kids will punch tickets and fun snacks can be served. The windows will be open, from which they hang out of almost to their waist waving to all that they pass. From here, you hear the great shrieks of delight and the thrills and excitement of rounding each bend.

The clickity-clack, clickity-clack can almost be visualized as you notice the children bopping up and down ever so slightly at each track connector. One child will surely shout out, "We need to stop for coal and watah!" only to be out-shouted by two or three others, "Go fastah, go fastah!" Remembering they are gnomes you might not be surprised to hear them ask in unison, "Can we go backwards?!"

The caboose is a highly revered vehicle to a select set of the more responsible gnome children. Only one or two will be allowed to be the conductor and carry out these important duties. Usually this is the smallest gnome. You'll see him leaning off the back steps waving the small lantern, "All clear, all aboard!" and the train will begin to chug. The caboose is also where the infamous safe is kept, well hidden from the would-be vandals and robbers who could be waiting just around the river bend. Here-in they also keep the highly prized mail which they must carry faithfully from station to station.

Who will be the engineer is anyone's guess. All gnomes want to be driving the powerful engine, with its giant wheels, powerful steam whistle, and endless dials and controls. Each will clamor first for this job, and there's no telling who's going to win. It seems that logic will prevail and one will better justify this right of responsibility.

The engineer is the boss. You will hear his strong voice

announcing today's theme for the train ride. It might be "Today, we're takin' ol' ninety-nine through Indian Country! There's great danger in hanging out them thar' windows. . The ing'ns are aftah your scalps and owr gold." Followed by, "We need all available hands stokin' the coal if we'se gonna outrun the band of Apaches."

Such are the experiences we've heard them recall from the many park rides we have taken them on, where they have great train ride adventures. Your experience will reflect your family and times with the gnomes and elves.

We took the children to the local hobby store to select the stations, trees, and stores to make their experience more complete and whimsical. Together, we chose water towers, loading docks, warehouses, logs, trees, and bridges to add to the authenticity of the themes. The school bell rings, the station-house lights up, and the switches divert cars to side tracks.

CHILDREN'S TOYS
In addition to model trains, which gnome children can play and imagine with for hours, a male gnome child also likes miniature cars, skateboards and wagons - basically anything with wheels. However, unless they have been taught how to ride a bike, they may be more skittish of bicycles.

Roller skating can be hilarious to watch, because they don't know how to turn, and they run into each other and fallover. Being gnomes and elves, skating backwards and up hill is a normal part of the fun. We've seen them skating in long chains, five or six at a time, some so short their skates don't touch the ground. Others have extra-large wheels which convey the ingenuity that the gnomes bring to their playtime.

The little girls have taken to, exceedingly so, the real workings of the miniature battery operated sewing machine. Mamma and Granny got into the event by influencing us to go shopping at the local sewing store for tiny 4-inch bundles of pre-cut fabric assortments tied in ribbon, ideal for the size and requirements of the gnomes, elves, leprechauns, and faeries alike.

Granny was herself captivated by the gnome-packs of two and three shiny brass buttons and crystal bobs. Mamma grabbed a small sewing box from the craft section so as to properly teach the young ladies the essence of their craft. It's only fair that if you treat the boys to realistic toys that the young girls must be suitably included.

Even the small gnome children are captivated by the colorful "Toys'We'Is" commercials.

They make the most of your proximity to these stores, subtly mentioning that, "We are by such and such," – and, "How come we nevah goes dar?" (You really have to wonder at this gnome synchronicity, hmm?)

Most adults would find these toy store mega-sites monolithic and foreign at first, but somehow curiously inviting once acclimated inside. Perhaps it's the child inside of them. Our children were first drawn to the coloring book racks and the pre-school book shelves. Their eyes were wide and bright, showing overwhelming excitement like "kids in an oversized candy store" when they sighted the mile-high mountains of toys, sets and kids stuff.

You will find it an especially happy place, one ideally suited to a short afternoon's entertainment for each and every one of your nature people children. While there, you will be surely drawn to toys that your children are particularly enthralled with. They may be charmed by the doll-sized furniture they can use or enamored with the bright red child-sized wagons with real rubber wheels.

Their imaginations are so enchantingly creative, that their minds work somewhat like ours in a dream state. You will observe amazing inventiveness in their sharing at play, and as the toys themselves become transformed into a veritable theme park. We remind people how watching gnomes and elves play demonstrates the ease at which solutions to problems can be produced when we are truly unlimited by our imagination.

"If you're gonna have kids, you're gonna have toys!"

"If you're gonna have kids, you're gonna have toys!"

-- So says gnome Everette

"Kids want the stuff that makes THEM feel like they're playin' in their dreams. These may not be your dreams. Deep down the kiddies might want to be a cowboy or cah-pentah, or a ball-a-rina. You gottah discovah what those magical dreams awr in your little kids, or you're going to loose touch with dem."

"The little kids are gonna have their play-time dreams no mattah what you tink. So if you wanta be part of their enjoyment, you need to observe, listen, an' understand what they'se telling and showing you. We'se can't always do it in specific words, so sometimes you have to feel for the answah. When you find that special kiddie connection, then we can start having fun. Let's go shoppin'!"

"Since you know now whether you need to take little junior gnome to the hobby store or fluffy bell fairy to the craft store, or jungle jim elf to the giant toy stores, the rest is gonna be easy. The moment the store is open, your gnome will leave two feet off the ground an' grab your hand an' scream loudly in your eah, 'This way Mommy! This way Daddy! Aisle six has the kiddie tool belts!' Or,

'They got the best block sets in the back of the store! We'se gots to hurry or we won't get all the letters that we need!'"

"You know when the gnomeses are happy, 'cause you'll feel our excitement inside of you. You'll just know. The most certain way is when you find yourself asking, 'Did you want anything else Billy?' If you have a bunches of gnomes an' elves then you should always take care of the elves furst. Hhahahh." Carson says.

Everette steps back in and says: "The elves wan the stuff on the top shelves, the gnomes wan the stuff on the bottom shelves, it just works out that way. The elves like to hide and seek in the store, so they can be a bit un-wrooley. They splashes us with watah guns when we'se trying to pick out owr toys. Then they run an' hide, laughin' at us."

Carson says, "'Cause we in this big playground of toys, we should be playin' with them too. You don't have to buy them 'till they announce the buzzer. Gnomes awr easy to watah squirt, 'cause they can't chase us up the mountains of toys, nearly as fast as we can climb. We get excited sometimes an' start pushin' down toys from the top shelf, an' say, 'Get this one too!' When the Mommies feel the toys fallin' next to them, that means the elves are makin' their suggestions. So there's no use arguin' about it. Just put the toys in the cart."

"Everette jumps back in, "When it's Christmas time, it's the best time to get the toys with wheels. Santa's had all year to fill up the tires so there's a full selection of bicycles an' little gnome cahs. You'll want to look at these carefully as they might bring particular joy an' happiness to your little one's. 'Hint. Hint.' You can always ask if you don't know the answah."

"If it's not Christmas yet, then you can buy the packages of little cahs, an' give each of your kids their own toy. If your little gnome boy wants to be a policeman like Billy, he's gonna want the little metal police car, with wheels that really roll an' a little red light on top. I like the little tractors an' fire engines."

"The girlies like different stuff. They got cooking sets for dem an' game cards an' clothes with glue on the back. They'se much easiah to shop for, 'cause of all the ninety-nine cent specials. The boys are more difficult 'cause you gottah find the right cowboy hat or doctah bag or tool kit that they want — cause they have dreams of being big people — an' they need to start practicing right away with their toys. The girlies just want babies, an' we'se already kids. So they'se a snap."

"All the boys' toys need batteries. That's why they'se on the counters ready for you to pick up in large quantities. These are sorted by age, 'A', 'double A' and 'triple A'. The little 'triple A' kids don't need as many batteries, but they charge more for their toys. So you may be only able to get them one. They like the toys with the noise. We'se biggah kids like the toys that move. The elves awr more strange, an' go for the educational sets. They nevah stop learning. An' girls just wanna have fun. So they don't need battery toys. They needs the ones that make them laugh an' make happy sounds 'cause their imaginations are tickled."

gifting the gnome

Love is a gift we can all give

— Grand Gnome Elder, Wasser-Sisser

"There is one Universal gift, and that is love. Love is the greatest gift of all because it is a never-ending, always generating force that can be partaken of to your capacity, and shared without limit."

"There are many aspects of Love for you to give. One is to give love from the heart. Know that we can feel this force and experience its boundless appreciation, the latter itself having great meaning. Sharing is an acknowledgement of the realms of Nature and the tireless effort we put forth for the wonderful evolution of Mankind. Acknowledge us in your lives and share your world with us."

"The aspect of Awareness is knowledge and there is much for you to know still. Open your minds to the realms of Nature and you will experience the greater meaning of life itself. We are here and we live in harmony with all life. We can help you find your missing note so that you too can blend perfectly with the music of Nature.

"Put this book under your pillow

... an' make a wish."

Peter-Jön's gift to you